Awakening

Challenging the Culture with Girls

Nurturing the
Spirituality of Girls

Awakening
Challenging the Culture with Girls

Janet Claussen

Voices:
Nurturing the
Spirituality of Girls

Saint Mary's Press
Christian Brothers Publications
Winona, Minnesota

The following authors contributed to this manual:
- Kat Hodapp, Louisville, Kentucky
- Julia Keller, Pebble Beach, California
- Danielle Rossi, Philadelphia, Pennsylvania
- Laurel Zimmerman, EdD, Minneapolis, Minnesota

Genuine recycled paper with 10% post-consumer waste.
Printed with soy-based ink.

The publishing team included Marilyn Kielbasa, development editor; Cheryl Drivdahl, copy editor; James H. Gurley, production editor and typesetter; Cindi Ramm, design director; Cären Yang, cover designer; back cover images copyright © Rubberball Productions; manufactured by the production services department of Saint Mary's Press.

Kendra Hengel, cover artist, Winona Voices Group, Winona, MN

Acknowledgments continue on page 135.

Printed in the United States of America

Printing: 9 8 7 6 5 4 3 2 1

Year: 2009 08 07 06 05 04 03 02 01

ISBN 0-88489-696-X

Library of Congress Cataloging-in-Publication Data

Claussen, Janet.
    Awakening: challenging the culture with girls / Janet Kohler Claussen.
        p. cm. — (Voices)
Includes bibliographical references.
ISBN 0-88489-696-X (pbk.)
        1. Church group work with youth. 2. Teenage girls—Religious life. 3. Catholic youth—Religious life.
4. Christianity and culture—Study and teaching. [1. Culture. 2. Teenage girls. 3. Catholics. 4. Christian life.
5. Conduct of life.] I. Title. II. Voices (Winona, Minn.)
BX2347.8.Y7 C53 2001
259'.23—dc21
                                                                                                2001001656

To my mother, Jeanie, my daughter, Katie,
and all other blessed women
who have awakened and nurtured me on the paths of life.

Contents

Introduction

"You are made in the image of God." That simple statement is the heart of spirituality—a profound statement about who we are and who we are becoming. There is no more important mantra for adults to communicate as they parent, teach, minister, and pray with young people.

The journey to adulthood has always been a time of transition. Those who walk with adolescents know that the journey is also unique for each person. In fact, recent studies confirm the age-old intuitive sense that girls and boys experience life in ways that are unique to their gender. If gender differences affect physical, emotional, and psychological development, then certainly, spirituality is shaped as well by feminine or masculine perspectives.

For girls in this country at the turn of the millennium, opportunities for equality are greater than for girls in any previous generation. Still, psychologists, educators, ministers, and parents know that the risks and issues that confront young females seem rooted in a different reality than those that face young males. Brought up in the crucible of a media world, girls continue to receive messages that beauty and body are more important than mind and spirit. Told that they can do anything, they too often engage in behaviors that endanger them more than empower them. In the interest of "being nice," they abdicate their voice to males, exhibiting a dramatic drop in self-esteem in their adolescent years.

Girls experience life in terms of relationships. While their male counterparts charge headlong into separation and independence, young women, by nature and nurture, seem predisposed to connectedness and intimacy. Psychologists like Carol Gilligan *(In a Different Voice)* and Mary Pipher *(Reviving Ophelia)* have brought attention to the life of girls, spawning an entire genre of literature aimed at addressing the phenomenon of the female adolescent experience. Addressing young women's psychosocial world is a good beginning, but few experts in the field of girls' development have ventured into the realm of spirituality.

Spirituality is about relationship—relationship with the One who created us. It is about loving and living out a call to become the kind of person God created us to be. Girls need to hear this message, embrace it, and live it. They need guidance to challenge a culture that contradicts their sacredness; they need adults who will listen to them, relate with them, and walk with them, reminding them of their destiny, reminding them, "You are made in the image of God."

"Herstory" of the Voices Project

The Voices Project is the realization of the dream of a national team of female educators, youth ministers, parents, and mentors who have a special concern for the spirituality of girls. They envisioned a multifaceted initiative that would bring together the energy of the girls' movement and the wisdom of women's spirituality. Their dream was a convergence of the work of psychologists Mary Pipher and Carol Gilligan with the work of Catholic writers like Maria Harris and Elizabeth Johnson. As a result of listening sessions with girls from around the country, the team identified the need for resources for adults who work with girls in Catholic school and parish settings. One response to that need is the Voices series.

Overview of the Voices Series

The Voices series consists of six manuals that present strategies to use with adolescent girls in schools, parishes, and single-gender settings. The authors and consultants in the series have extensive experience working with girls in both coed and single-gender situations. The manuals they have produced are different from one another in content and focus, yet all share the same purpose: to help girls embrace the true meaning of the phrase "created in the image of God," a profound statement about who they are and who they are becoming. This manual, *Awakening: Challenging the Culture with Girls,* is one of the results; the other manuals in the series are as follows:

- *Retreats: Deepening the Spirituality of Girls* presents seven retreats on themes such as friendship, media, and childhood myths. Also included is a retreat for mothers and daughters.
- *Prayer: Celebrating and Reflecting with Girls* provides ideas for community prayer services and suggestions for enriching girls' personal prayer life.
- *Church Women: Probing History with Girls* outlines strategies for discovering the richness of women's contributions to the life of the church.
- *Biblical Women: Exploring Their Stories with Girls* suggests ways to help girls get to know the women in the Scriptures and examine the roles they played in communities of faith and the beginnings of the church.
- *Seeking: Doing Theology with Girls* offers methods for exploring and discussing theological and moral issues from the perspective of women.

Where and When to Use the Voices Series

The Voices resource manuals can be used in a variety of settings, though they are intended for use with girls in single-gender groups. The rationale for meeting in single-gender settings is particularly compelling for young women. Numerous studies indicate that girls are much more likely to speak up, express their opinion, and be genuinely heard in "just girl" groups. Some topics related to growing up and finding one's way in society are difficult for females to discuss in the presence of males. Imparting the particular wisdom of women to girls, and of men to boys, is a time-honored practice that can be highly effective when used occasionally in educational, church, and social institutions.

Finding opportunities for single-gender gatherings can be a challenge; consider these suggestions:

- Offer gender-specific electives within a school or parish catechetical setting.
- Work with Scout groups, which are already gender specific.
- Form "just girl" groups that meet beyond the typical school day or parish youth night.
- Establish weekly or monthly sessions within the school or parish schedule, at which girls and boys discuss related topics separately. Subsequent discussion with both groups together can lead to greater understanding between the sexes.
- Create mother-daughter or mentor-mentee discussion groups.
- Organize diocesan days for "just girls" or "just boys," or both.
- Arrange retreats and youth rallies that have gender-specific components or workshops.

Who Might Use the Voices Series

The six resource manuals in the Voices series may be used by coordinators of youth ministry, directors of religious education, teachers in Catholic schools, campus ministers, youth ministers in parish settings, Girl Scout and Camp Fire leaders, parents, mentors, and other adults who work with girls ages ten to nineteen. Flexible enough for single-sex groups in any setting, the manuals' ideas are designed to engage girls in both headwork and heart work, challenging them to think while nurturing their spirit.

Overview of This Manual

Providing the foundation for all the other manuals in the Voices series, *Awakening: Challenging the Culture with Girls* focuses on opening the eyes of girls to recognize elements of the culture that keep them from fully becoming the persons God created them to be. Raising their consciousness can empower girls to resist negative pressures while developing healthy relationships with their self, others, and God.

How to Use This Manual

The themes in this manual can be used interchangeably and in any order. However, we strongly suggest that the first theme, "Voices and Choices: Challenging the Culture of Childhood Myths," be used as a foundation for the others. Likewise, the last theme, "Transforming Women: Promoting a Culture of Conversion," can provide a powerful conclusion and much food for thought at the end of a series of meetings or classes.

We do not expect that you will do all the material in every theme. Each theme is extremely flexible, providing a buffet of optional servings rather than a formal multicourse meal.

The first seven themes of the *Awakening* manual focus on challenging particular aspects of the prevailing culture, while encouraging countercultural ways of thinking that nurture the spirit of girls. The last three themes focus on promoting healthy attitudes about self and relationships. Each of those last three themes is based on a full-length feature film available at most video stores; the film and activities can be used over several group or class meetings, or for half- or full-day sessions or retreats. All the themes are formatted as follows.

Springboard Activities

Each theme contains one, two, or three springboard activities, designed to take 40 to 55 minutes each. These fully developed activities use a reflection method that begins with personal experience, progresses through analysis and critique, and closes with further action or exploration.

Additional Activities

Most themes include one or more additional activities outlined in detail. These activities provide good follow-up for the springboard activities and allow for age-appropriate assimilation of the material.

Actions and Options

Each theme also includes quick ideas for follow-up activities, adaptations for different age-groups, multigenerational interaction, service options, and social action.

Reflection and Discussion

Each theme presents suggestions for writing in journals, connections with the Scriptures, and quotes by and about women.

Prayers

Each theme offers one or two prayers related to its topic, which can be used to begin or end the theme.

Resource Materials

Most themes provide a list of resources—print, video, and Internet—for more exploration.

Background Information

The first six themes provide background information on their main issue. This material is based on research in the subject area and is given to help you guide the girls in their discussion and exploration of the topic.

Notes

Space is provided for you to jot down ideas, reminders, and additional resources as you use the theme materials.

Handouts and Resources

All the necessary handouts and resources for a theme are found at the end of the theme.

How to Get Started

Know the Material

Read each theme or activity before you facilitate it, and use it creatively to meet the needs of your particular group of girls. In particular, look for ways to make the material most accessible for the girls' ages and for the size of the group. Most of the suggestions in this manual can be used with girls ages ten to nineteen. Some material is most appropriate for a specific age-group within that span; in many cases, we have included recommendations for adapting such material for older or younger adolescents. Most of the activities in this manual are designed for groups of twenty to thirty young people, but can easily be adapted for any size group.

Know the Young People

When you have a wide variety of ages together, keep in mind the following differences between young adolescents and older teens:

- Young adolescents think in concrete terms and may not yet be capable of considering some topics abstractly. For example: Older adolescents will probably not have any difficulty recognizing the ambiguously subtle-but-transforming presence of the main character in the movie *The Spitfire Grill.* Young adolescents will have a much easier time recognizing the obvious effect of the main character on other characters in *Beauty and the Beast.*
- Young adolescents generally need more physical movement than older teens do. You can address that need through simple activities such as forming small groups for discussion and moving to different halves of the room to indicate the answer to a yes-or-no question.
- When they are working in small groups, young adolescents do better with an adult or older teen leading them. Groups of older teens can often be left alone for discussions.
- Older teens can usually handle open-ended assignments, but young adolescents respond better to writing exercises and discussions if they are led. For example, a junior in high school can be expected to write a letter to God about a certain topic on a blank sheet of notebook paper, whereas a sixth grader will be more focused with sentence-starters to guide different parts of the letter.

Create a Welcoming Environment

When possible, adapt the physical space to allow for open discussion and sharing. Consider moving chairs into a circle or inviting everyone to sit on the floor, at times. Groups that meet regularly may want to create a sacred space for ritual, using candles, fabric, music, favorite statues, sculptures, and images. Encourage the girls to be involved in creating that space and keeping it special.

Create a Safe Environment

When involving mothers, mentors, and other adults, provide written guidelines and even training in group leadership to help them understand the process and dynamics of the group. Consider the following guidelines for any adults who work with the group:

- To hear girls at the level necessary for meaningful interaction, adults need first to listen to themselves and to remember their own adolescence (Patricia H. Davis, *Beyond Nice*, p. 119).
- Girls need adults who will listen to them and affirm them even when their questions and actions seem uncomfortably challenging, and adults who will allow themselves to be questioned at deep levels (p. 120).
- Girls need confidentiality in any group that engages them in deep thinking, feeling, and sharing. Yet they and the adults who lead them also need to know when to go beyond the resources of the group to seek help.
- Girls need adults who will help them be countercultural in ways that bring animation and love to their life, their community, and their world (p. 121).
- To help girls recognize and nurture their own relationship with God, communities of faith need to listen to and learn from them and take them seriously, with engaged hearts, minds, and souls (p. 121).

Foundational Resources

The Girls' Movement

Gilligan, Carol. *In a Different Voice: Psychological Theory and Women's Development.* Cambridge, MA: Harvard University Press, 1993. This scholarly book is the foundation for Gilligan's later works, which emphasize the unique psychological and moral perspective of girls and women.

Girl Scout Research Institute, Girl Scouts of the USA. *Girls Speak Out: Teens Before Their Time.* Executive summary. New York: Girl Scout Research Institute, Girl Scouts of the USA, 2000. This publication explores issues ranging from relationships and physical development to gender roles, among girls ages eight to twelve. It is available from Girl Scouts of the USA, 420 Fifth Avenue, New York, NY 10018-2798, *www.girlscouts.org/news/GSRINews.htm.*

Phillips, Lynn. *The Girls Report: What We Know and Need to Know About Growing Up Female.* New York: National Council for Research on Women (NCRW), 1998. Commissioned by the NCRW, this text is a comprehensive summary of research that looks at almost every aspect of life for girls. Available through the NCRW, 11 Hanover Square, New York, NY 10005, 212-785-7335 (phone), 212-785-7350 (fax), *www.ncrw.org.*

Pipher, Mary. *Reviving Ophelia: Saving the Selves of Adolescent Girls.* New York: Ballantine Books, 1995. A clinical psychologist, Pipher uses the voices of adolescent girls to tell their stories of loss of self, depression, eating disorders, and lowered expectations.

Feminine Spirituality

Anderson, Sherry Ruth, and Patricia Hopkins. *The Feminine Face of God: The Unfolding of the Sacred in Women.* New York: Bantam Books, 1991. A landmark book on women's experience of God, faith, and religion.

Chittister, Joan D. *Heart of Flesh: A Feminist Spirituality for Women and Men.* Grand Rapids, MI: William B. Eerdmans Publishing Co., 1998. This book explores a new way of being in the world based on circles rather than pyramids, compassion instead of competition, and a new kind of feminism rooted in Gospel values.

Davis, Patricia H. *Beyond Nice: The Spiritual Wisdom of Adolescent Girls.* Minneapolis: Fortress Press, 2001. Using a base of one hundred in-depth interviews with girls from a variety of religious, ethnic, and regional backgrounds, the author conveys the deepest spiritual concerns of girls as they try to ground and affirm the women they are becoming.

Harris, Maria. *Dance of the Spirit: The Seven Steps of Women's Spirituality.* New York: Bantam Books, 1989. This classic work about women's spirituality is useful for both individuals and women's groups that wish to engage in exercises of self-discovery that lead to transformation.

Schneiders, Sandra M. *With Oil in Their Lamps: Faith, Feminism, and the Future.* New York: Paulist Press, 2000. In this text of her lecture delivered as part of the Madeleva lecture series at Saint Mary's College, Notre Dame, in 2000, Schneiders makes a strong case for Gospel feminism as a way to bring out the full humanity of all persons.

Your Comments or Suggestions

Saint Mary's Press wants to know your reactions to the strategies in the Voices series. We are also interested in new strategies for use with adolescent girls. If you have a comment or suggestion, please write the series editor, Marilyn Kielbasa, at 702 Terrace Heights, Winona, MN 55987-1320; call the editor at our toll-free number, 800-533-8095; or e-mail the editor at *mkielbasa@smp.org.* Your ideas will help improve future editions of these manuals.

Part A

Challenging Negative Cultures

Voices and Choices

Challenging the Culture of Childhood Myths

Springboard Activity

Losing Your Voice, Getting Your Man

This activity introduces the psychological and social world of girls as dramatized in the Walt Disney version of the classic story "The Little Mermaid." Through an analysis of the film, the girls learn to critique the myths and stories of the culture. The activity is designed to raise the girls' consciousness about a culture that expects them to sacrifice their identity by giving up their voice and changing their body, as Ariel does in the film. The activity is appropriate for both middle school and high school audiences.

Preparation

○ Review and bring in the Walt Disney film *The Little Mermaid* (1989, 83 minutes, rated G).

1. Divide the girls into small groups. Tell the groups each to list on a sheet of paper their five favorite children's animated movies. When they are done, gather everyone and create a Top 5 list by writing down all the movies identified by the small groups, using slash marks to note how many lists each movie appeared on, and circling the five movies that were included on the most lists. You can hold a vote to break a tie if one occurs.

2. Introduce *The Little Mermaid* by asking one of the girls to summarize its plot. Identify the following main characters: Ariel, the fifteen-year-old mermaid; Eric, the human prince she loves; and Ursula, the evil sea witch. Invite the girls to share any special memories of watching the movie as a child. Then show the clips described below.

- *Clip 1 (about 20 minutes into the movie, about 3 minutes long).* Following an argument with her father, Ariel brings a fork to her secret cave to add to her treasures, and sings "Part of Your World."
- *Clip 2 (about 37 minutes into the movie, about 10 minutes long).* After angry words with her father, who has forbidden her to go near the land where Eric lives, Ariel is upset. Ursula lures Ariel to her cave with the help of Flotsam and Jetsam, her accomplices. Eventually, Ariel emerges from the water to begin her quest for Eric.

3. Lead a discussion around questions like these, comparing the first and second clips:
- What changes about Ariel's appearance? personality? interests?
- Why does Ariel change?

4. Ask the girls to recall the lyrics to "Poor Unfortunate Souls." Consider dividing them into small groups again and seeing which group can come up with the most accurate lyrics, recording them on newsprint. Check the recalled words against the lyrics in the film. Post the lyrics; clarify any words or phrases that raise questions.

5. Discuss the song lyrics in one large or several small groups, by posing questions like the ones that follow:
- What lines does Ursula use to convince Ariel to give up her voice? Do her words disturb you? Why or why not?
- Is there any truth to Ursula's arguments?
- Is it true that men do not care about what a woman has to say?
- Do you think that girls change in order to attract boyfriends? If so, what are some ways that they change?
- Do girls and women talk too much about silly things?
- Ursula tells Ariel that life is full of tough choices. What are the pros and cons of Ariel's choice?
- What do you think of Ariel's decision? Do you think that most girls would have made the same decision if, like Ariel, they did not know how it would turn out? Why or why not?

6. End the discussion in a large group with questions like these: "Do girls in middle school or high school change when they are around boys in the classroom or in social settings? If so, in what ways?" Use the background information near the end of this theme to report what some experts say about the topic.

7. Close the activity by asking the girls what God might say to Ariel about her situation. Light a candle and invite the girls to take turns giving Ariel one bit of advice in the name of God. You might also have them each write a letter to Ariel from God.

Additional Activities

Children's Fairy Tales

This activity works with middle school and high school girls as long as the level of discussion is age appropriate. Younger girls may have some trouble with the last step; if that is the case in your group, provide examples to get them started.

Preparation
○ Bring in the original Hans Christian Andersen story "The Little Mermaid." Ask a librarian to recommend other children's stories that have strong roles for girls, and bring in those as well.
○ Ask the girls to bring in books and stories that they enjoyed as children.

1. Conduct this activity as a story hour. If possible, have everyone sit on the floor, and invite the girls to remember childhood experiences of story time. Read Andersen's version of "The Little Mermaid" aloud to the group, showing them any illustrations.

2. Compare the Disney animated version of the story with the original Andersen fairy tale. Then pose questions similar to these:
- Is the mermaid's decision in the Andersen story more difficult than the choice that Disney's Ariel has to make? Why or why not?
- What kind of sacrifices do traditional gender roles ask women to make? What kind of sacrifices do men make?

3. Invite the girls to share the books and stories they brought and what they liked about them. Examine the following issues:
- Invite the girls to point out the books and stories that have girls as main characters. Then ask them to describe the personalities or characteristics of any girl protagonists in those works.
- If there are few young heroines in the books and stories, discuss why and explore how the girls feel about that.
- If time allows, ask volunteers to read from their books and stories selections that portray strong role models for girls.

4. Close the activity by asking the group how they think society would be different if most little girls heard stories about young women who are strong and independent, instead of weak and dependent as they are traditionally portrayed in most fairy tales.

A Hollywood Talk Show

In this exercise, the girls act out a talk show episode in which movie studio executives explain their positions to an audience that asks pointed questions about the roles of women and girls in animated movies. This activity works best with high school girls.

Preparation

○ Post the group's Top 5 animated movies from the springboard activity for this theme. If you did not do that activity, complete just step 1 of it and post the resulting Top 5 list.

○ Gather the video covers from as many of the movies on the Top 5 list as possible, and use them to decorate the meeting space.

○ Arrange four chairs in the front of the room.

○ Make four signs that can be worn around the neck and label them, "Host," "Director," "Producer," and "Screenwriter."

1. Recruit four girls who are familiar with most of the movies on the Top 5 list, to be a host and a panel of Hollywood movie moguls on a TV talk show. Assign each person one of the roles identified on the signs you made; give each recruit the appropriate sign to wear and a copy of resource 1, "Talk Show Scripts"; and allow the four girls a few minutes to prepare their parts.

Tell the rest of the group that it will be the studio audience. Provide seven members of the audience each with one of the questions from resource 2, "Talk Show Questions." Explain that those questions may be used to start the discussion or move it along, and that anyone in the audience may also ask their own question whenever the host invites discussion.

2. Call the host to begin the discussion, and help her keep the show moving until all the guests have made their introductions and everyone has had an opportunity to ask questions.

3. Ask the group to comment on how they feel about the way that girls and women are portrayed in children's movies. Extend the discussion to the portrayal of girls and women in movies for teens and adults.

Mothers and Daughters

As part of this gathering, you may want to show all or part of the film *The Little Mermaid II,* in which the theme of mother-daughter relationships is prominent. However, the activity does not rely on the film; if you choose not to use it, skip step 4 of the activity procedure.

This activity is appropriate for both middle school and high school audiences. Middle school girls are more likely to be able to engage in a discussion of the topic after seeing the film, so if your group consists of primarily younger teens, be sure to include the movie.

Preparation

○ Ask the girls each to invite to the session their mother, a grandmother, an aunt, or another woman they admire and consider a mentor.

○ Review and bring in the Walt Disney film *The Little Mermaid II: Return to the Sea* (2000, 75 minutes, rated G).

1. Gather the girls and their guests in separate groups. Be sure that each group has a sheet of newsprint and some markers, or paper and pencils. Challenge the groups to see which one can list the greatest number of pairs of famous mothers and daughters from world history, the Bible, church history, movies, television, and literature. Allow about 10 minutes for this task.

2. Invite each group to share its list with the other. The groups may need to explain some of the pairs. They may also want to describe the kind of relationship each mother-and-daughter pair had.

3. Discuss questions like these:
◉ How easy or difficult was this task?
◉ Would it have been easier if you had been asked to list famous fathers and sons?
◉ What have you learned about women losing their voices and about the roles of women in society and history?

4. Show *The Little Mermaid II*. Afterward, offer the following comments in your own words:
◉ At the beginning of the film, Ariel, now a human mother, saves her daughter, Melody, from the clutches of Morgana, Ursula's sister. [Point out some important elements of the dialogue in the story, such as mothers not understanding their daughters and mothers wanting their daughters always to be a part of them.] The climax of the movie centers around Ariel's decision to rescue the adolescent Melody from the perils of evil lurking in the sea.
Discuss the role of mothers in helping girls avoid the dangers and pitfalls of growing up, when it might be appropriate for mothers to rescue their daughters, and when parents should let girls make their own mistakes.

5. Invite insights and affirmations about the power of mother-daughter relationships. Conclude with a blessing service of the girls and their guests.

Creative Voices

This activity can be done with girls in middle school or high school. Younger girls may need a little help getting started, but once they have an idea, they will find a way to work it out. The projects may be completed in small groups, as described, or assigned to individuals or pairs.

Divide the girls into small groups. Assign each group one of the following media, or invite the groups to choose one for themselves: skit, video, children's book, music, and dance. Explain that each group is to use its medium to tell girls ages six to nine about the importance of using your voice and staying true to yourself. When the projects are completed, invite each group to present its creation to the others. You might also arrange for the girls to present their projects to younger girls.

The Sound of Voices

This activity works best with groups of eight or more girls. It can be used as an ice-breaker or within a session, to help the girls get to know one another as they focus on the importance of their voices.

Preparation

○ Ask the girls each to make a 1- to 2-minute audio recording describing their voice—that is, their power to influence others. You might want to set up a tape recorder in another room, give each girl a blank tape, and send the girls in one at a time to make their recording. Emphasize that they should not identify themselves in any way on the recording, but they should write their name on the cassette.

1. Collect all the tapes and, without identifying the speakers, play them for the group. Lead the girls to identify the speaker in each case. You might encourage the speaker to keep a low profile while the others are trying to identify her.

2. When every voice has been identified, offer the following sentence-starters and invite the girls to share their responses:
   ◉ Something I learned about myself by doing this activity is . . .
   ◉ Something positive I learned about someone else is . . .

Options and Actions

- Suggest that the girls commit to reading regularly to a group of children in their school or parish. Help them select books and stories that have strong girls in leading roles.
- Education gives people a voice and control over their choices. Nearly 54 percent of girls worldwide will never enter primary school, and of those who do, fewer than half will stay in school through fifth grade (Education Now, Oxfam America). Find out more about the status of girls and women in the global community through resources like the Girls Global Education Fund, *www.ggef.org/issues.html*.
- Find out what Catholic church leaders say about the role of women, by reading some of the resources listed at *www.nccbuscc.org/opps/current/women.htm*.
- Encourage the girls to check out Web sites that promote healthy self-esteem. These sites have links especially appropriate for middle school girls: *www.girlsinc.org*, *www.health.org/gpower*, and *www.newmoon.org*. The site *www.smartgirl.com* is more appropriate for older adolescent girls.
- Play songs from animated movies and critique the lyrics with the girls. If any concerns surface, as a group, write an article about them for your school or local paper, and send a copy to the music publisher and movie studio.
- Form a support group for girls to help one another maintain a positive self-image, use their voices, and make good choices.

- Assign each girl to write a review of a children's book that illustrates a positive role model for girls. Send the reviews to local elementary schools, libraries, and newspapers.
- Provide art materials and encourage the girls each to make a poster that shows who they are right now—using only pictures and symbols, no words except their name. Invite everyone to share their completed posters and explain the symbolism. Decorate your meeting space with the posters.

Reflection and Discussion

Journal Questions

- What movies, books, or toys were your favorites when you were growing up? Which influenced you? How did they affect your sense of the way girls live?
- Describe a time when you chose silence in the face of strong pressure from others. Also describe a time when you chose to speak out in the face of strong pressure.

Scriptural Connections

These passages from the Gospels offer examples of women with strong voices:
- Matt. 15:21–28 (the Canaanite woman)
- Luke 10:38–42 (Mary and Martha)
- John 4:7–30 (the Samaritan woman at the well)
- John 20:1–18 (Mary Magdalene)

WomanWisdom Quotes

'Tis woman's strongest vindication for speaking that *the world needs to hear her voice.* It would be subversive of every human interest that the cry of one-half the human family be stifled. (Anna Julia Cooper)

Nobody can make you feel inferior without your consent. (Eleanor Roosevelt)

Human rights are not worthy of the name if they exclude the female half of humanity. The struggle for women's equality is part of the struggle for a better world for all human beings, and all societies. (Boutros Boutros-Ghali)

It was Christ who discovered and emphasized the worth of woman. It was Christ who lifted her into equality with man. It was Christ who gave woman her chance, who saw her possibilities, who discovered her value. (Arthur John Gossip)

Too many women in too many countries speak the same language—silence. (Anasuya Sengupta)

To validate a young girl's voice, it is essential that we make the act of listening to her a conscious, significant act. How we listen and attend to her will help shape her own sense of significance. (Tim Hinds Flinders and Carol Lee Flinders)

Prayer

Jesus, strong and gentle friend, you treated everyone with great love and respect. In a time when women were supposed to be silent, you talked with them, you healed them, and you encouraged them to use their voices. You even chose them to spread the good news of your Resurrection. Empower us to use our voices in ways that will help all people to become the persons they were created to be, made in the image of God. Amen.

Resource Materials

Print

Golden, Stephanie. *Slaying the Mermaid: Women and the Culture of Sacrifice.* New York: Three Rivers Press, 1998. The author uses the Hans Christian Andersen story "The Little Mermaid" to critique the culture in which women have been taught to sacrifice themselves for others at great expense to their own well-being. An adult resource, this book poses challenging questions about age-old assumptions of gender roles.

Kolbenschlag, Madonna. *Kiss Sleeping Beauty Good-Bye: Breaking the Spell of Feminine Myths and Models.* Garden City, NY: Doubleday, 1979. This work by a Catholic sister surveys old myths to break the spell of feminine myths and models. The author chooses Belle of the fairy tale "Beauty and the Beast" as a model for today's authentic heroine.

Background Information

Studies of the psychological and social world of girls—such as *Reviving Ophelia,* by Mary Pipher, *In a Different Voice,* by Carol Gilligan, and *Girls Speak Out,* by the Girl Scout Research Institute—indicate that girls experience a significant drop in self-esteem beginning with preadolescence. Those studies confirm that the identity work of adolescent girls differs from that of their male counterparts. Girls often undergo a transformation from being strong, capable, and happy with themselves to being insecure about self-expression, body image, and leadership abilities.

The "loss of voice" combined with the pressure to conform to the norms of a sexual culture often result in eating disorders, depression, lowered expectations, and increased sexual activity among girls. Several studies from the 1990s indicate that girls receive less attention in the classroom than do boys, and that during the middle school years, there is a significant drop in self-esteem among girls. According to one study: "Girls aged eight and nine are confident, assertive, and feel authoritative about themselves. Yet most emerge from adolescence with a poor self-image, constrained views of their future and their place in society, and much less confidence about themselves and their abilities" (American Association of University Women, *Shortchanging Girls, Shortchanging America,* p. 7). According to Pipher, "Girls have long been trained to be feminine at considerable cost to their humanity" and "everywhere girls are encouraged to sacrifice their true selves" (p. 44).

Children's movies illustrate the reality of expected gender roles that contribute to this loss of identity. Boys and men are often cast as authority figures or as romantic love interests to be pursued at the cost of self. Girls and women are seldom portrayed in roles that exhibit their intelligence, leadership, or strength. Beauty and charm are more important than intelligence and independence. Strong older women are often portrayed as evil, and there is generally an absence of relationships with mothers, mentors, friends, or sisters.

Romantic infatuation generally drives the story line, and the heroine finds fulfillment in living happily ever after with her man. Because girls are naturally inclined toward forming close relationships, they are more prone to stereotypical messages that are often unhealthy for the development of their own identity.

The concern about girls is not limited to the psychological and social worlds. Their spirituality, the very essence of their person, is affected by this culture that encourages them to be silent and passive. However, it is in the realm of spirituality that girls can be nurtured and empowered to address issues of self-identity. By introducing girls to the Gospel message that both men and women are made in the image of God, we can promote healthy attitudes of self. And we can encourage girls to speak up and speak out, knowing that Jesus affirmed the power of women's voices through his conversations and interactions with women in a time and place that often silenced them and put them on a par with animals, property, and slaves (Exod. 20:17).

Notes

Use this space to jot ideas, reminders, and additional resources.

Talk Show Scripts

Host

Your job is to introduce the topic and guests for the episode "Girls' Voices in the Movies." Also, you are to call on the audience to ask your guests questions. Feel free to ad-lib and be creative with your role, while keeping the discussion going like a professional talk show host.

Use this script to introduce yourself, your guests, and the topic of this episode:

My name is _____ [name]. Today, on my show, *GirlPower Talks,* I have with me three media experts from Hollywood: Director _____ [name], Producer _____ [name], and Screenwriter _____ [name]. They are going to address our questions about male and female roles in children's animated movies.

Now, my guest experts will tell the audience a little about what they do, and perhaps pick their favorite children's movie from your list of Top 5 favorites.

Select one of the three experts to go first. After the expert's introduction, choose individuals from the audience to ask any of the questions your leader passed out or questions of their own that relate to today's topic.

Director

Read the following introduction when you are asked to do so:

My role in moviemaking is to direct the voices, the facial expressions, and the body language of the characters. I determine how sweet, mean, silly, serious, or intelligent a character might come across as to the audience.

Producer

Read the following introduction when you are asked to do so:

My role model was Walt Disney himself. Now, I decide what movies are worth making and which ones I think will sell in the marketplace to kids and their families. I control the money and resources to make the film.

Screenwriter

Read the following introduction when you are asked to do so:

I make up stories, or adapt fairy tales or popular stories, for animated films. As the writer, I usually have the freedom to change a story to make it appeal to today's audiences.

Talk Show Questions

On the Top 5 list created by your group, which movies involve an absent mother and a young adolescent girl?

Are there any animated movies that show a strong, supportive human mother or other woman who is a positive role model in a girl's life?

Are there any animated movies in which girls have strong friendships with other girls? If so, how significant are those friendships?

How are older women portrayed in the movies listed?

How are boys and men portrayed in the movies listed?

Where do most of the ideas for those movies come from?

Can you think of any children's stories of strong girls?

Male and Female, God Created Them

Challenging the Culture of Gender Stereotypes

Springboard Activities

Yin-Yang

Using the ancient symbol of the yin-yang and contemporary scholarship, this activity helps the girls explore gender differences from psychological and historical perspectives. They also examine the connection between those perspectives and their own spirituality. This activity is particularly appropriate for high school girls.

Preparation
○ Create a large yin-yang from black and white fabric. Use the diagram below as a model.

○ Type or print each of the following terms onto a separate large adhesive mailing label. The words should be large enough for the young women to see from a distance. Divide the labels into three or four relatively equal stacks.

emotional	intimate	abstract
static	creative	a follower
intuitive	thoughtful	masterful
strong	romantic	self-interested
merciful	omnipotent	vengeful
trusting	objective	practical
mutualistic	patient	sharing
nonviolent	feeling	realistic
liberating	communal	personal
cooperative	decisive	public
logical	sensual	responsible
empowering	empathetic	compartmentalized
challenging	tough	passive
materialistic	hospitable	assertive
concrete	rational	independent
a leader	dynamic	scientific
a servant	intellectual	tender
selfless	vulnerable	organized
forgiving	just	manipulative
visionary	controlling	subjective
possessive	territorial	honorable
mysterious	violent	thinking
political	competitive	individualistic
private	oppressing	divisive
compassionate	artistic	sexual
connected	overpowering	weak
active	nurturing	sentimental
aggressive	spiritual	honest

1. Explain the symbolism of the yin-yang using the following information. Then ask the participants how they feel about the characteristics attributed to the feminine side of the yin-yang.

  ◉ "Yin and yang are two principles in Chinese philosophy. Yin represents the negative, passive, feminine, earthly component of the universe, characterized by darkness and weakness. Yang represents the positive, active, masculine, heavenly component, characterized by light and strength. The yin-yang symbol illustrates the balance that exists between these two complementary components. It uses a circle divided by a wavy line into two curved forms, one dark and one light. The dark side represents the yin, and the light side represents the yang" (adapted from Jeffrey Brodd, *World Religions,* p. 138).

2. Divide the girls into three or four groups. Give each group a stack of characteristic labels. Explain the task as follows, in your own words:

- ◉ Discuss the quality on each label and decide whether society primarily associates it with women, men, or both. Do not get into "should" or "would," but rather focus on how society actually views the quality. Put the labels into three stacks: feminine, masculine, and neutral.

3. After the girls finish deciding, ask someone from each group to peel one label off its backing and place it on the yin-yang where they think it belongs, according to the following guidelines:

- ◉ The black area is for feminine qualities. The white area is for masculine qualities.
- ◉ Qualities you consider to be extremely feminine or masculine should go near the outside edges.
- ◉ Neutral qualities should go on or near the wavy centerline—the closer to the line, the more gender neutral the quality.

4. Once all the labels are affixed to the yin-yang, ask the girls to decide if they agree with the placements. If they do not, help them come to consensus about where the labels do belong, and move them accordingly.

5. Lead everyone in a discussion focused around questions like the ones that follow:

- ◉ Do you think that these stereotypical gender qualities are the result of nature or nurture? That is, are we born with a tendency toward feminine or masculine traits, or does society mold them into us?
- ◉ Is it good or bad that women and men tend to have different qualities?
- ◉ Do you see yourself as possessing both feminine and masculine traits?
- ◉ Do you think that if boys or men had done this exercise, the results would have been different? If so, how?

Invite further comments or insights about the exercise.

6. Conclude with the following remarks in your own words:

- ◉ It seems clear that gender differences exist, but in reality, both females and males possess what we term feminine and masculine qualities. God has created the feminine and the masculine, the yin and the yang, to be in right relationship with each other.
- ◉ Masculine gifts should never be valued more than feminine gifts. Nor should traditionally feminine qualities be important only in private places like home and family. As individuals and as a society, we need to be aware of the beauty and value of both the masculine and the feminine aspects of humanity.

Gender Attitude Survey

This survey gives the girls a chance to take a stand on various issues and let others know the reasons for their choices. It is appropriate for both middle school and high school girls and should generate some lively discussion.

Preparation

○ Make four signs, each with a different one of the following responses, and post one in each corner of the room:

a. I strongly agree.

b. I agree.

c. I disagree.

d. I strongly disagree.

○ Write the numbers 1 to 10 each on a separate piece of paper. Fold the papers and put them in a container.

1. Distribute handout 1, "Gender Attitude Survey." Give the girls about 3 minutes to fill in the survey. Tell them not to put their name on their sheet.

2. Ask a volunteer to draw a piece of paper from the container and announce the number to the group. Tell the girls to look at their answer for the statement with that number, and to move to the corner of the room with the corresponding sign.

When every girl has committed herself to a corner of the room, invite the group to discuss their responses. Use the background for leader comments at the end of this activity to explain any gender study findings that apply to the statement.

Move on to the next statement by asking a volunteer to draw another number. Complete as many statements as possible in the time you have available.

3. Present the following ideas in your own words:

◉ "Because there are physical, emotional, and intellectual differences between men and women, it makes sense that women have a different perspective on the world of faith, religion, and spirituality. However, because of *patriarchy,* meaning 'rule by the fathers,' theology and spirituality have been seen through the perspectives of men.

"Sexism hurts both men and women, and we are called to change our hearts about traditional ways of a world in which men have dominated. God created us as male and female to reflect the wholeness of God. We are all made in God's image" (adapted from Renew International, *Renewing for the Twenty-first Century,* pp. 22–23).

4. Distribute handout 2, "Male and Female, God Created Them." Divide the room in half and call the two halves to read alternate lines of the poem.

Background for leader comments

1. *Boys play competitive games more than girls do.* Studies about the behavior of small children confirm that boys like to play competitive, aggressive games more than girls do. They also are concerned more with the precise rules of the game. Girls prefer to quit the game when an argument happens (Carol Gilligan, *In a Different Voice,* pp. 9–10).

2. *Girls like to play indoors more than boys do.* Carol Gilligan's research reveals that boys are more likely to want to play outside, engaging in very physical games. Girls tend to play quieter, less physically aggressive games (pp. 9–10).

3. *Women talk more than men do.* Deborah Tannen, in her book *You Just Don't Understand,* says that women may talk more in private, but men talk more in public—at meetings, in mixed-gender discussions, and in classrooms where girls sit next to boys (p. 75). She goes on to say that men engage in "report" talk and women in "rapport" talk. Men like to exhibit knowledge, skills, and problem solving; women establish connections and negotiate relationships while comparing similarities and matching experiences (p. 77).

4. *It is more acceptable for a woman to show her emotions than for a man to do so.* This statement reflects stereotypical cultural norms that expect boys and men to keep more sensitive emotions under control. Psychologists who work with boys say that boys are born with the potential for a full range of emotional experience. However, as boys get older, they express less emotion—with the possible exception of anger (Dan Kindlon and Michael Thompson, with Teresa Barker, *Raising Cain,* pp. 10–11). Girls, on the other hand, often have trouble expressing anger, which demonstrates their fear that anger disrupts friendships (Tannen, p. 259).

5. *It is more exciting to watch boys play sports than to watch girls play sports.* This is a purely subjective issue that will generate strong opinions. A good connection is that often, girls' sports are not funded as much as boys', nor do girls get the same kind of attention in schools, communities, and the media. Title IX laws that require equal funding of male and female sports in school are often not implemented. What do the girls in your group think of those inequalities?

6. *Boys are more physically aggressive than girls are.* Dramatic statistics confirm that boys and men, as a group, are more physically aggressive and violent (Kindlon and Thompson, p. 219). Why? Does the culture promote violence through movies, video games, and toys that are marketed to boys? Do girls and women find violence less acceptable?

7. *Girls are better at language arts than boys are.* Educational psychologists concur that girls' verbal abilities, on average, mature faster than boys' do. Later in school, however, boys tend to catch up with language arts. Studies of gender difference in math performance show that overall, girls tend to do slightly better in the early school years (Kindlon and Thompson, p. 12). However, in the middle school years, girls decide in greater numbers that they do not like math. Only one in seven high school girls report that they are good at math. One in four boys say the same thing (American Association of University Women, *Shortchanging Girls, Shortchanging America,* p. 11). Like all gender differences, those do not apply to all individuals. However, they are a good basis for discussion about whether girls tend to do better in some subjects than in others. Does the culture discourage girls from liking math and science, or is disliking those subjects a natural tendency?

8. *Adolescent girls have different attitudes about sex than adolescent boys do.* There is an old saying that women give sex in order to get love, men give love in order to get sex. While that may be stereotypical, it is a biological fact that boys are more easily aroused than girls are and that in our sex-saturated culture, boys have sex on their mind a lot (Kindlon and Thompson, p. 196). A recent study of over two thousand girls revealed that girls want to learn to say no to sex and still say yes to intimacy (Pamela Haag, *Voices of a Generation,* p. 28).

9. *Girls worry more about relationships than boys do.* The background information near the end of this theme provides some of the psychological reasons why girls and women are drawn more toward intimacy and men more toward independence. You might ask the girls if they can think of personal experiences that exemplify that phenomenon.

10. *Girls are more involved in religious activities than boys are.* The girls can address this statement from their own observation and experience of church, youth ministry, Bible study groups, and prayer groups. In addition, any casual count of a Catholic faith community usually reveals a majority of women in attendance at Mass and in parish organizations. Studies show that 75 percent of active Catholics and 80 percent of laypeople working for the church are women.

Options and Actions

- As a follow-up to the first springboard activity, have the girls reflect on gender balance in their own life. Create a handout with a large yin-yang diagram and give each girl a copy. Ask the girls to look at the characteristics on the group yin-yang from the first springboard activity, and to write the ones that apply to them in the appropriate half of their yin-yang diagram. Invite them to share their personal yin-yangs with one another.

   Point out that like being right- or left-handed, or thinking in their native language, most people prefer either their masculine or their feminine side, but it is healthy to develop qualities from both halves of the sphere.

- Challenge the girls to create a yin-yang for their ideal mate. Ask them to think about what qualities they would like to see in someone they might date or marry. Encourage them to compare the result with their own yin-yang.

- Ask the girls to finish these sentences:
   - I'm glad that I am a girl because . . .
   - If I woke up tomorrow and discovered that I was a boy, I would . . .

   Discuss their answers, and invite them to ask several boys to finish the same sentences, changing the gender words.

- Direct the girls to label a sheet of paper with two categories: "Ways I have benefited from being a girl today" and "Ways that I have not benefited from being a girl today." Tell them to jot down examples under each category for the next several days. After several days, have the girls compare lists, noting the gender differences that they have observed and discussing any insights they have gained. (This activity is adapted from Tim Hinds Flinders with Carol Lee Flinders, *Power and Promise*, p. 206.)

- Suggest an interdisciplinary project that examines the voices of women in various academic subjects. Ask the girls how many women mathematicians, scientists, artists, or writers they have studied. Suggest that they examine the indexes in their school textbooks—including their religion textbook—to see how many women's names are listed.

- Do a media review with the girls, looking for stereotypical gender roles in television shows, movies, and commercials. Write letters to studio and station executives, voicing concerns about perpetuating stereotypes.
- Encourage the girls to interview women and ask their opinion about gender differences and how roles have changed during their lifetime. Suggest that the girls video- or audiotape their interviews and share them with the group.
- Recommend that your group conduct a gender attitude survey with girls who are eight or nine years old. They can use handout 1 as a basis, changing the questions as necessary to suit the younger audience.
- Help your group design bumper stickers, buttons, T-shirts, or a graffiti board, with slogans that affirm the value of both women's and men's gifts.
- Encourage the girls to research Internet sites that promote the strengths of women.
- Assign small groups to create skits that portray both effective and ineffective communication between men and women about common topics like sports, movies, sex, and religion. Guide the group in critiquing the skits based on what they have learned about gender differences.
- Read the story of the wedding feast at Cana, John 2:1–11. Reflect with the girls on how Jesus and Mary exhibit masculine and feminine characteristics at that celebration. Note these things: Jesus expresses his need for independence, and Mary reacts out of concern for relationship. Jesus and Mary respond to each other with mutual respect. It is God's design for there to be harmony between the sexes:

> God created humankind in [God's] image,
>
> . . . .
>
> male and female [God] created them.
>
> (Gen. 1:27)

Reflection and Discussion

Journal Questions

- Reflect on the benefits and advantages of your being a girl. What are some of your hopes and dreams for the kind of woman you feel called to be?
- Reflect on how gender roles affect understanding and misunderstanding between boys and girls, and men and women. Identify an occasion when it could be beneficial to understand how women and men might think differently about the same topic.
- Think of some of the most balanced people you know—male and female. Using a yin-yang, plot out the qualities in them that the world considers to be masculine and that the world says are feminine.

Scriptural Connections

- Gen. 1:26–27 (We are all created in the image of God.)
- 1 Cor. 12:12–31 (We are all important in the Body of Christ.)
- Gal. 3:28 (We are all one in Christ Jesus.)

WomanWisdom Quotes

Originally, woman was the sun.
She was an authentic person.
But now woman is the moon.
She lives by depending on another
and she shines by reflecting
another's light.

. . . . . .

We must now regain our hidden sun.

. . . .

"Rediscover our natural gifts!"

(Hiratsuka Raicho)

If a woman can only succeed by emulating men, I think it is a great loss and not a success. The aim is not only for a woman to succeed, but to keep her womanhood and let her womanhood influence society. (Suzanne Brogger)

[Woman] has swung between these two opposite poles of dependence and competition. . . . Both extremes throw her off balance; neither is the center, the true center of being a whole woman. She must find her true center alone. She must become whole. (Anne Morrow Lindbergh)

The sexes in each species of beings . . . are always true equivalents—equals but not identicals. (Antoinette Brown Blackwell)

But the heart . . . of all traditional feminine initiations . . . lies in the imparting of traditionally feminine skills: life-sustaining skills like spinning, weaving, knitting, pottery, cooking, healing, gardening . . . and of course worship itself, the maintenance of an open line with the sacred. . . . To have such skills *is* to enter the adult community. (Carol Lee Flinders)

Prayer

Woman was not a powerful word before.
No one's head would turn when a girl walked through the door.
They were not considered strong, independent, or even daring.
Women were always supposed to be motherly, loving, and most of all, caring.
Now things have changed.
Since Amelia, the first woman to fly a plane,
and Rosa Parks, who stood for her rights because she knew that it was only sane.
With those strong women and many more,
they were the women who opened many doors.
For the power of God was shown through all of them;

God showed them they were created equal to men.
So each little girl that reads this now,
Show the one who created you that you are **strong** and ***proud***.
Let the women in the future be heard and always taught,
that many other women have paved the way,
to let all little girls be heard and have a say.

(Beth Cunningham, "Women: Past—Present—Future")

Background Information

by Janet Claussen and Julia Keller

The field of developmental psychology involves the study of how we, as humans, develop in thought and behavior. That serves as a good starting point for looking at basic differences and similarities between men and women.

Traditionally, psychological tests and theories, which measure how we develop in thoughts and actions, have been based on all male subjects, and have been conducted and developed by all male theorists. Freud, a psychologist in the early twentieth century, provides a prime example. He, and many who followed him, concluded that, based on the male psychological model of "normal" development, women did not develop normally, or were somehow less developed than their male counterparts. Not until later in the twentieth century did people begin to wonder, Just because women do not develop in the same way as men, does that mean that they are not normal? New studies and theories focusing on female subjects have revealed that women are not lacking in psychological development, but develop differently, along different lines (Carol Gilligan, *In a Different Voice*, pp. 1–7).

Carol Gilligan, who has done a great deal of work on the subject of women's psychological development, cites a 1974 study by Nancy Chodorow that specifically investigates the developmental psychology of women. In the study, Chodorow points out that women are usually responsible for child rearing during at least the first few years of a child's life. During that time, mothers and daughters relate and identify with each other as "like" creatures, as women. Mothers and sons, on the other hand, realize that they are different. Part of their natural task, therefore, is to separate, to become more independent; as the "opposite sex," they must differentiate and become opposite. Gilligan says:

> Since masculinity is defined through separation while femininity is defined through attachment, male gender identity is threatened by intimacy while female gender identity is threatened by separation. Thus males tend to have difficulty with relationships, while females tend to have problems with individuation. (P. 8)

In other words, from the time of birth, a girl's task is to relate, and a boy's task is to separate. Therefore, Chodorow argues that girls begin life with more built-in empathy and sensitivity toward relationships than boys do (pp. 7–8).

Gilligan goes on to cite a 1976 study in which Jane Lever follows schoolchildren at play. That study supports the premise that girls continue to value relationships over independence and differentiation. Boys choose to play competitive games that require a high degree of skill, like soccer or baseball. In Lever's study, when disputes arose in the game, the boys did not hesitate to squabble and fight. But interestingly, they never chose to end the game because of a dispute; at worst, they would repeat the play to settle it. Gilligan says, "In fact, it seemed that the boys enjoyed the legal debates as much as they did the game itself" (p. 9). Girls, on the other hand, are more likely to play turn-taking, noncompetitive games like hopscotch and jump rope. In playing their games, girls tend to be more flexible on rules, and "more willing to make exceptions" (p. 10). Most interestingly, girls are more likely to end or quit a game if a dispute breaks out—the relationships are more important to them (p. 10).

Another interesting psychological difference between men and women is observed during the teenage years. According to traditional psychological models, that is a time when people are supposed to develop identity and independence, and prepare for their entrance into the adult world of productivity and work. Gilligan sees that to be true of teenage boys. But teenage girls, she points out, often follow a different course of development, resisting an individual identity in favor of future relationships. Although that is changing in our current society, it can still be seen in women's roles and expectations. Men always have a constant self-defined identity: they retain their family name throughout their life, and they create a sense of self through their independent place in the working world. Women, on the other hand, are constantly defining themselves through their relationships—they often take their husband's name, and for at least part of their adult life, their primary priority may be the bearing and raising of children, which keeps them out of the workforce at least long enough to give birth and recover. Gilligan cites a study that draws a correlation between the fairy tales of Sleeping Beauty and of Snow White, and what is actually happening to young girls in adolescence: they spend their teenage years blissfully asleep until they are awakened by their prince, whom they will marry (p. 13).

Gilligan also cites studies showing that as women break into adulthood, and more often these days into the professional world, they continue to value relationships more than men. In 1972, Matina Horner found that women in the workplace exhibited "anxiety . . . about competitive achievement" (p. 14). In Horner's study, women were anxious about being successful if their success was dependent on another person's failure. In a corporate, capitalistic environment, a fear of competitive achievement is in fact defined as a fear of success. Gilligan and others suggest that there are other, broader definitions of success.

What is clear from all these studies is that women value relationship over individuality and cooperation, while men value individuality and competition over relationship. Neither is "wrong" or "right." But clearly, men and women are different from a developmental perspective.

Helping girls to recognize gender differences can lead them to greater self-understanding and better communication with males. Perhaps most important, it can lead girls to a better understanding of what influences their gender identity and how healthy it is to seek gender balance. In fact, studies show that girls who exhibit both feminine and masculine attributes have higher levels of self-esteem than do girls who most strongly endorse an exclusive feminine gender orientation. The girl who describes herself as both caring and competitive, both nurturing and assertive, seems most likely to remain self-confident throughout adolescence (Susan Harter, as reported in Tim Hinds Flinders with Carol Lee Flinders, *Power and Promise,* p. 36).

Because spirituality is at the very essence of the human person, psychologically and socially, developmental differences are important to spiritual growth as well. The human experience mediates spirituality, and therefore, the experience of women and girls influences their spiritual worldview. As girls approach the study of God, human relationships, and the church, they will benefit spiritually from perspectives that affirm both masculine and feminine qualities.

Notes

Use this space to jot ideas, reminders, and additional resources.

Gender Attitude Survey

After reading each of the following statements, circle the response that best represents your reaction to it.

1. Boys play competitive games more than girls do.
   - *a.* I strongly agree.
   - *b.* I agree.
   - *c.* I disagree.
   - *d.* I strongly disagree.

2. Girls like to play indoors more than boys do.
   - *a.* I strongly agree.
   - *b.* I agree.
   - *c.* I disagree.
   - *d.* I strongly disagree.

3. Women talk more than men do.
   - *a.* I strongly agree.
   - *b.* I agree.
   - *c.* I disagree.
   - *d.* I strongly disagree.

4. It is more acceptable for a woman to show her emotions than for a man to do so.
   - *a.* I strongly agree.
   - *b.* I agree.
   - *c.* I disagree.
   - *d.* I strongly disagree.

5. It is more exciting to watch boys play sports than to watch girls play sports.
   - *a.* I strongly agree.
   - *b.* I agree.
   - *c.* I disagree.
   - *d.* I strongly disagree.

6. Boys are more physically aggressive than girls are.
   - *a.* I strongly agree.
   - *b.* I agree.
   - *c.* I disagree.
   - *d.* I strongly disagree.

7. Girls are better at language arts than boys are.
   - *a.* I strongly agree.
   - *b.* I agree.
   - *c.* I disagree.
   - *d.* I strongly disagree.

8. Adolescent girls have different attitudes about sex than adolescent boys do.
   - *a.* I strongly agree.
   - *b.* I agree.
   - *c.* I disagree.
   - *d.* I strongly disagree.

9. Girls worry more about relationships than boys do.
   - *a.* I strongly agree.
   - *b.* I agree.
   - *c.* I disagree.
   - *d.* I strongly disagree.

10. Girls are more involved in religious activities than boys are.
    - *a.* I strongly agree.
    - *b.* I agree.
    - *c.* I disagree.
    - *d.* I strongly disagree.

Male and Female, God Created Them

Leader: God, you created all of us. Male and female, in your image, you created all of us. Help us to live out our call to be your reflection in this world.

Side 1:   For every woman who is tired of acting weak when she knows she is strong,
there is a man who is tired of appearing strong when he feels vulnerable.

Side 2:   For every woman who is tired of acting dumb,
there is a man who is burdened with the constant expectation of "knowing everything."

Side 1:   For every woman who is tired of being called "an emotional female,"
there is a man who is denied the right to weep and to be gentle.

. . . .

Side 2:   For every woman who is tired of being a sex object,
there is a man who must worry about [being macho].

Side 1:   For every woman who feels "tied down" by her children,
there is a man who is denied the full pleasures of shared parenthood.

Side 2:   For every woman who is denied meaningful employment or equal pay,
there is a man who must bear full financial responsibility for another human being.

Side 1:   For every woman who was not taught the intricacies of an automobile,
there is a man who was not taught the satisfaction of cooking.

Side 2:   For every woman who takes a step toward her own liberation,
there is a man who finds the way to freedom has been made a little easier.

(Nancy R. Smith, "For Every Woman," in *Images of Women in Transition*, compiled by Janice Grana [Winona, MN: Saint Mary's Press, 1991], page 49. Copyright © 1976 by The Upper Room, Nashville, Tennessee. All rights reserved.

That Was Then, This Is Now

Challenging the Culture of Sexism

Springboard Activity

Those Were the Days

The topic of sexism is key to this activity, in which the participants explore issues that pertain to the cultural and spiritual lives of girls and women. The activity gives the girls a chance to compare traditional roles of women against today's norms, introduces historical changes in church and society, encourages analysis and critique of the status quo, and empowers the girls to reflect on their own roles in all areas of their life. Leaders of this theme should be sensitive to both positive and negative aspects of the changing roles of girls and women.

Preparation
○ Cut green, yellow, and red construction paper into 2-by-3-inch strips. Each girl will need one strip of each color.

1. Distribute handout 3, "How to Be a Good Wife," to all the participants. Read the handout aloud while the girls follow along. Then discuss questions like these:
- What is your impression of these instructions for women?
- What ideas from the reading stand out for you—either positively or negatively?
- From what you have read and heard from older women, do you think that most married women in the 1950s followed these guidelines?
- How might these guidelines have affected boys and men in the 1950s?
- Do you think that boys in the 1950s received instructions about how to be a good husband?

2. Give each girl one green, one yellow, and one red strip of paper. Explain that you will read a series of statements. They are to vote by raising the appropriate color strip, as follows:

- Green means, "I agree."
- Yellow means, "I'm not sure."
- Red means, "I don't agree."

Read the following statements. After each one, scan the votes for general agreement or disagreement, and discuss any statement that generates a difference of opinion.

- Women and men are equal.
- Women should be paid the same amount for the same work as men.
- Women should have the same opportunities for education as men.
- Women should be able to vote.
- Women should be able to own property.
- Women should be able to have a credit card in their name.
- Women can be strong leaders.
- Women can be principals, heads of companies, politicians, doctors, construction workers, lawyers, and auto mechanics.
- A woman can be president of the United States.
- Women and men should share the responsibility of raising children.
- Women and men should share the responsibility of earning a living.
- Women should be able to serve in the military, even in combat roles.
- Women's sports should be given the same amount of financial support as men's sports.
- Girls should be allowed to play football on a team.
- Boys should be encouraged to be cheerleaders.
- I consider myself a feminist.

3. Make the following points in your own words:
- Most of the rights for women that I just named were gained in the United States in the last century, starting with the right to vote in 1920. Much has changed since then. In the 1960s, the women's movement pushed for equal rights in many of the areas I mentioned.
- In 1968, the term *feminism* was defined as "the doctrine advocating social and political rights for women equal to those of men" *(The Random House Dictionary of the English Language)*.
- Most men and women in the United States today would agree that women and men are equal, but the term *feminism* is still controversial for both genders.

4. Form pairs or triads. Explain that each girl has 2 minutes to explain to her partner or partners what she likes or dislikes about the term *feminism* and how she might change its definition if she were to write the entry for a dictionary published this year. Monitor the time while the participants complete this task.

5. Gather the girls and solicit some of their ideas for ways to change the definition of the word *feminism*. Share with the group the definition of the term *Gospel feminism* given by Sr. Sandra M. Schneiders: the "Gospel vision of full humanity for all persons and right relations among all creatures" (*With Oil in Their Lamps*, p. 116). You may want to add that Gospel feminism calls women and men to prophesy a culture of life, rejecting the violence of abortion, the death penalty, the gun lobby, and euthanasia (see the background information at the end of this theme). Then make the following points in your own words:

◉ Sister Schneiders' definition of *Gospel feminism* is rooted in the message of Jesus, who was faithful to his religious tradition. However, Jesus did not hesitate to challenge his world with a clear vision of the Reign of God.

◉ As disciples of Jesus, we too are called to live the Gospel and strive to be in right relationships with one another and with the earth.

Invite the girls to comment on the differences between the dictionary definition of *feminism,* their own definitions of *feminism,* and the definition of *Gospel feminism.*

Additional Activities

Change Is Good—or Is It?

This activity challenges the girls to identify the changes that have happened for women in the last century and to evaluate their positive and negative impacts. It is most appropriate for older teens.

Preparation
○ Cut red, yellow, and green construction paper into 2-by-3-inch strips. Each girl will need one strip of each color.

1. Ask the girls to brainstorm changes that have occurred for women in the last one hundred years in business, careers, education, family life, public life, sports, school, church, and entertainment. List the changes on newsprint or the board.

2. Give each girl one red, one yellow, and one green strip of paper. For each item on the newsprint or board, ask the girls to vote with their slips of paper as follows:
◉ Red means, "This was a bad change for women."
◉ Yellow means, "I'm not sure about this change."
◉ Green means, "This was a good change for women."
Tally the results and put the totals next to each item.

3. Give each girl one red and one green self-stick dot. Explain that the participants are to place their red dot next to the change they think did the most harm to women, and their green dot next to the change that did the most good for women.

4. Look over the results of both voting sessions. Comment on items that evoked significant agreement or disagreement, and invite the girls to do the same. If you have time, conduct another round of voting and discussion to explore whether the changes were good or bad for men.

Changing Times

This activity should generate a lot of discussion as the girls explore some controversial aspects of feminism. It is most appropriate for older teens.

Preparation
○ Make enough copies of resource 3, "Changing Times," for every six to eight girls. Cut apart the questions as scored and keep the questions from each copy of the resource together as a set.

1. Make the following points in your own words:
◈ Gender roles have changed more in the last one hundred years than in the five thousand years before. There have been so many changes in just a couple of generations that some people—male and female—may wish to go back to the "good old days." Change is often difficult for individuals, but it is even harder for large communities and societies. This activity allows you to talk about some of the complex issues that arise as gender roles change.

2. Divide the girls into groups of six to eight and direct each group to form a circle. Place a set of questions from resource 3 facedown in the middle of each circle.

3. Recruit someone in each group to begin the exercise, and explain the process as follows:
◈ The recruited person will pick a card, read it silently, and decide if she wants to answer it. If she does not like the question, she may return it to the pile and pick another, but she must answer the second question. She should read the question aloud to the group and answer it, then return it to the pile. Others may then voice their opinion, but we must keep the discussion moving so that everyone has a chance to answer a question.
You may want to appoint someone in each group to keep the exercise moving.

4. When everyone has answered at least one question in their group, gather the girls and pose questions like these:
◈ Which question or questions generated the most discussion in your group? the most consensus? the most disagreement?
◈ Were there any questions that people seemed reluctant to talk about? If so, why were those questions difficult?
Conclude by pointing out that many men, as well as women, support gender equality, and that many women, as well as men, are content with the old inequalities.

Then and Now

This activity uses quotes from a variety of church leaders to help the girls explore how the church's attitude toward women has changed and has been articulated through the ages. It is particularly appropriate for older teens, though many younger girls may be able to understand its significance.

Preparation

○ Copy resources 4, "That Was Then," and 5, "This Is Now," onto two different colors of paper. Cut apart the quotes as scored. Make enough copies so that you have one quote for each girl, with half the group getting quotes from resource 4 and half from resource 5.

○ To establish the proper atmosphere, you may want to create a ritual for reading the quotes that includes a centering space and quiet music.

1. Randomly distribute the quotes and form two groups according to the color of the quotes. Ask the groups to stand or sit in two rows, facing each other.

2. Call the girls to read the quotes seriously and prayerfully. Invite someone from the "That Was Then" group to begin by reading her quote aloud, ending with the refrain, "That was then." Someone from the "This Is Now" group should then read her quote, beginning with the statement, "This is now." Alternate readers from each group until all the quotes have been read.

3. Encourage the girls to talk about their reactions to the quotes. Discuss the changing roles of women in the church and the attitudes of church leaders toward women throughout history. You might ask questions such as these:

◎ How has the church leaders' perception of women changed throughout history? How has it remained the same?

◎ Has the church influenced society's attitudes toward women? Has society influenced the church's attitudes toward women?

◎ How active is the Holy Spirit in guiding women and men of faith to a "Gospel vision of full humanity for all persons and right relations among all creatures."

Inclusive Language

Based on the premise that language is powerful, this activity introduces the concept of inclusive language as it reflects changes in society. This exercise is appropriate for both younger and older teens.

Preparation

○ Find a hymn that uses mostly male imagery, such as "Faith of Our Fathers." Locate another hymn that uses inclusive language, such as Ruth Duck's "Womb of Life, and Source of Being" (available from GIA Publications) or Bernadette Farrell's hymn "God, Beyond All Names" (available from Oregon Catholic Press). Both types of songs can be found in typical parish hymnals. If possible, get enough copies of the hymns for all the girls.

○ Choose one quote from resource 4 and one from resource 5. Write the quotes on newsprint or the board.

1. Explain that you will now read the lyrics of two songs. Ask one-third of the girls to keep a running list of all the words and phrases associated with men, one-third to do the same for words associated with women, and one-third to keep track of words or phrases that include both men and women. If the girls do not have copies of the hymns, you may need to read the lyrics more than once.

2. Invite the groups to share their lists with everyone. Talk about the images, when the songs were written, what changes have occurred in the use of language, and other pertinent information. Emphasize that when older hymns were written, male imagery was the norm and the concept of gender fairness was not an issue.

3. Define the following terms:

• *Exclusive language.* language that identifies as male or female mixed groups, inanimate objects, persons whose gender is unknown, and God
• *Inclusive language.* language that avoids identifying as male or female mixed groups, inanimate objects, persons whose gender is unknown, and God

Discuss with the girls some of the reasons to *avoid using* exclusive language. Also refer to the quotes you have written on newsprint or the board, as you present and explore these reasons to *use* inclusive language:

֎ Language shapes and is shaped by thought. The language we use can help bring about changes in society. For example, as attitudes about civil rights have changed over the years, we have changed the way we refer to people of color to be more sensitive. Degrading terms for ethnic groups contribute to discrimination and are also a sign of it.

֎ Using inclusive language acknowledges the sexist bias of the English language and confronts the attitudes of a patriarchal society. At one time, the words *men* and *mankind* meant only "males." For example, the well-known phrase in the Declaration of Independence, "All men are created equal," referred only to white men who owned property. If the same document were to be written today, no doubt, it would state clearly that men and women are created equal.

֎ Inclusive language, sometimes called gender-fair language, allows people to say exactly what they mean—no more, no less. Consider a bowl of apples and oranges. What one word describes its contents? The answer is *fruit*. It would not be correct to describe the contents as only apples or only oranges. The same concept holds true for a room of girls and boys: we would call its contents people, not only girls or only boys.

Gender Fairness Takes Practice

1. Pair the girls, and give each pair handout 4, "Inclusive Language Is Gender Fair." Announce the following instructions in your own words:

֎ Everyone will now get a chance to practice making language inclusive. With your partner, you are to rework each word, phrase, or sentence on the handout to include both men and women, while remaining true to its original meaning. Write each new statement under the old one.

2. Go through the completed handouts as a large group. Then lead a discussion, focused around questions like the ones that follow:

- ⚬ Which words, phrases, or sentences were most difficult to change?
- ⚬ For which words, phrases, or sentences did you come up with multiple options?
- ⚬ Can you think of any other common statements that could be changed to help shape a new way of thinking?
- ⚬ Are there any settings or times in which inclusive language might be inappropriate?

3. Close the activity by challenging the girls to be aware of hearing and using noninclusive and sexist language, such as using the phrase "you guys" to mean everyone. Emphasize that we should always try to use language in a way that is respectful and fair to both genders.

Sexism in the Scriptures

This activity gives the girls a chance to wrestle with some of the negative images and sexist ideas in the Scriptures. It is most appropriate for high school girls.

1. Give each person a Bible and ask everyone to turn to Sir. 25:13—26:18. Skim the passages, noting that they were written in a patriarchal culture that had very different standards for men and women. You may want to define the terms *sexism* and *patriarchy*, using material from the background information at the end of this theme.

2. Create five small groups and give each group a sheet of newsprint and markers. Assign each group one of the following passages:
- Sir. 25:13–19
- Sir. 25:20–26
- Sir. 26:1–9
- Sir. 26:10–12
- Sir. 26:13–18

Explain that each group is to rewrite its passage on the newsprint so that it describes a man rather than a woman, using the same style and similar language, and drawing parallels as much as possible. For example, "Do not be ensnared by a woman's beauty, / and do not desire a woman for her possessions" (Sir. 25:21) could be rewritten as "Do not be ensnared by a man's good looks, / and do not desire a man for his possessions."

3. When the groups are finished, call them together to read the whole passage with its new twist. Then invite discussion about the images that language creates and the stereotypes that we promulgate when we do not interpret even sacred writings in the context of the time and place they were written. Make the following points in your own words:
- ⚬ "We have to remember that the Bible was written by human beings and reflects their cultural standards. The attitude of the writer of the book of Sirach was commonly accepted in his culture. But the cultural standards in the Bible do not always reflect God's truth. That is why we need the help of the larger

church community to properly interpret the Bible. Today, the church teaches that women and men are to be treated with equal dignity and respect. Let's work together with all men and women of God to continue making that vision a reality" (adapted from Saint Mary's Press, *The Catholic Youth Bible*, p. 810).

(This activity is adapted from Christine Schmertz Navarro et al., "Sexism Reversal.")

Options and Actions

- Many people over the age of fifty have clear memories of what life was like before the women's movement. Invite older women to join your group in a "Fifties Day" session to explore role-playing a 1950s home economics class with the teacher conducting a lesson on how to be a good wife. Proceed with variations of the springboard activity.
- Instruct the girls to interview a grandparent or other older person who can remember growing up in a more sexist world, and to ask what they see as the positive and negative aspects of changing gender roles. Consider directing the girls to audiotape their interviews and present clips to the group.
- Direct the girls to rewrite the instructions from handout 3 for today's typical family, and to title the new handout "How to Be a Good Spouse."
- Research the work of artists like Mary Cassatt and Judy Chicago. Bring in examples of their work and discuss how women have changed the world of art. You might invite a local artist to give her perspective on the impact of women. Provide art materials and invite the girls to create images that convey their feelings about being a young woman in society today.
- Direct the girls each to explore how sexism exists in literature, art, history, science, math, or music.
- Obtain old dictionaries from as far back as possible. Have the girls look up the words *sexism, feminism, patriarchy,* and *inclusive language.* Ask, "How recently did those words appear as standard in English?"
- Ask the participants to keep a list of exclusive and sexist language that they hear during the next week. At the end of the week, invite everyone to share their lists. Discuss what the girls think of these examples in light of what they have learned in this theme.
- Urge the young people to close their eyes and think about what they see and hear when they go to Mass. Then invite them to imagine what it would be like if they belonged to a church where the worship leaders were women, the service was offered for the salvation of all women, the readings were addressed to "my sisters in Christ," and ritual passages used phrases like "women of God." Ask them how such a church would influence the girls and boys who grew up in it, society, and the church members' sense of God. Finally, encourage them to draw conclusions about the effects of predominantly male language and images in the faith life of a community and its male and female members.

Reflection and Discussion

Journal Questions

- What are the positive and negative aspects of growing up female in the twenty-first century, compared with growing up female in earlier times?
- How is God calling you to change society? How do you feel about that?
- How do you feel about all you have learned about gender-fair language? What impact has such language had on you?
- With whom and how will you share what you have learned in this theme?

Scriptural Connections

- Gen. 1:27 (God creates humankind in God's image.)
- Wis. 7:22–30 (The nature of wisdom in female images)
- Matt. 28:1–10 (Jesus appears to two women and tells them to announce the good news of his Resurrection.)
- Luke 1:46–47 (The beginning of the prayer known as the Magnificat)
- Gal. 3:27–28 (There is no longer male or female.)

WomanWisdom Quotes

It is time for the woman. It is time to talk and set things right, for women to stand up. And when the world honors women, the mothers, and Mother Earth, everyone will be better off. (Cecilia Mitchell)

Language is neither innocent nor neutral. Linguistic habits condition our view of the world and hinder social change. (Carmen Martínez Ten)

Language conveys a certain power. It is one of the instruments of domination. It is carefully guarded by the superior people because it is one of the means through which they conserve their supremacy. (Sheila Rowbotham)

Sexism goes so deep that at first it's hard to see; you think it's just reality. (Alix Kates Shulman)

It is interesting that many women do not recognize themselves as discriminated against; no better proof could be found of the totality of their conditioning. (Kate Millett)

Prayer

Creator God, who made us all in your image, help us to imagine a world where all people are in right relationship with one another. Empower us to move beyond our imagination to walk with one another, bringing the good news of Jesus' message, the Reign of God, to all men and women on this earth. Amen.

Resource Materials

Print

Ashe, Kaye. *The Feminization of the Church?* Kansas City, MO: Sheed and Ward, 1997. The author of this book analyzes key issues of spirituality, ethics, morality, language, ministry, and leadership from the perspective of women in the church today.

Schaffran, Janet, and Pat Kozak. *More Than Words: Prayer and Ritual for Inclusive Communities.* New York: Crossroad, 1986. The introductory material of this text provides solid background and practical ideas on gender-fair language. Of particular note is a lengthy list of inclusive names for God, using a variety of images.

Background Information

Human experience mediates spirituality, that is, our relationship with God. Like all relationships, spirituality is situated within the context of the world in which we live. The cultural roles of girls and boys, and women and men, may have some genetic basis, but the expectations and norms of society have a large influence as well.

From biblical times, girls and women have had few rights of their own. Once considered property, women have been valued and affirmed as daughters, wives, and mothers of men, whom they have served. Patriarchy has been the norm of society, with men dominating governments, businesses, academia, and religious institutions while women primarily influence what happens in the home.

In many parts of the world, girls are still valued less than boys, receive little or no education outside the home, and are subject to the authoritarian rule of their father, brother, or husband. However, in the last one hundred years, much has changed for girls and women in the United States. There has been a great upheaval in society since the controversial suffragettes won the right to vote in 1920. In the 1960s, the women's movement called for equal rights for women and men. As a result, laws were changed to provide equal opportunities for girls and women at all levels of society, and attitudes of sexism grounded in thousands of years of patriarchy began to change.

But change often means controversy, and feminism has become a touchy subject. Many people feel that it has led to the controversial issues of the sexual revolution, increased rates of abortion, divorce, and troubled children raised in day care and in latchkey homes.

The church has been affected as well. Women theologians now teach at universities and seminaries, where once they were excluded. Ministries within the church have opened up, and the wisdom of women's spirituality has enriched the faith lives of women, men, and children, ordained and lay. Pope John Paul II, in his encyclical *The Gospel of Life* (*Evangelium Vitae,* 1995), refers to a "new feminism" that acknowledges and affirms "the true genius of women in every aspect of the life of society." That new feminism challenges women to reject the temptation of imitating models of "male domination," overcoming "all discrimination, violence, and exploitation" (no. 99).

The pope and others have called for a critique of the "old feminism," which made great gains for girls and women but took some wrong turns. If women were to be successful in a man's world, they had to become like men rather than transforming the world of men. Old feminism's emphasis on individual freedom, expressed as "It's all about me" and "It's my choice," has contributed to a culture that disregards the communal nature of human behavior. Sex without consequences has actually led to greater exploitation of girls and women, who feel pressured to be sexually active without the commitment of marriage. As abortion was legalized, it contributed to the further disconnection of sex from its life-giving potential.

As women and men of faith look to the future, new models and definitions of feminism continue to challenge them. In the year 2000, a group of fifteen women theologians and spiritual writers met at Saint Mary's College, Notre Dame, to envision and write a message of hope and courage for women of the future. The term *Gospel feminism* emerged from the lecture of Sr. Sandra M. Schneiders and became a key phrase as the women imagined a future that reflected the design of God. The manifesto of that enlightened gathering issues an invitation to the young women of the church:

> Walk with us as we seek to follow the way of Jesus Christ, who inspires our hope and guides our concerns. The Spirit calls us to a gospel feminism that respects the human dignity of all, and who inspires us to be faithful disciples, to stay in the struggle to overcome oppression of all kinds. . . .
>
> . . . We ask you to join us in a commitment to far-reaching transformation of church and society in non-violent ways. (Madeleva Manifesto)

Gospel feminism calls women and men to prophesy a culture of life, rejecting the violence of abortion, the death penalty, the gun lobby, and euthanasia. Patricia McGuire, in her address at the 25 March 2000 Jubilee Day for Women, said that if we believe in the gospel of life, we must speak out against social conditions that mock that gospel, raising our voices loudly and insistently about the ethical and moral dimensions of technology that can undermine or even destroy the human spirit and soul ("Transforming the Political and Social Discourse of Our Times").

The issues of feminism and women's equality are different for young people today than for their parents and grandparents. But more than ever, the world calls for women and men of faith who will be concerned not just about equality but about transforming the world for God's children and all of creation.

Notes

Use this space to jot ideas, reminders, and additional resources.

How to Be a Good Wife

This excerpt is adapted from an article in the 13 May 1955 issue of *Housekeeping Monthly*. It illustrates how Americans were living out their roles in family life.

Have dinner ready. Plan ahead, even the night before, to have a delicious meal—on time. This is a way of letting him know that you have been thinking about him and are concerned about his needs. Most men are hungry when they come home and the prospect of a good meal is part of the warm welcome needed.

Prepare yourself. Take fifteen minutes to rest so that you will be refreshed when he arrives. Touch up your makeup, put a ribbon in your hair and be fresh looking. He has just been with a lot of work-weary people.

Be a little gay and a little more interesting. His boring day may need a lift.

Clear away the clutter. Make one last trip through the main part of the house just before your husband arrives, gathering up school books, toys, papers, etc. Then run a dust cloth over the tables. Your husband will feel he has reached a haven of rest and order, and it will give you a lift too.

Prepare the children. Take a few minutes to wash the children's hands and faces (if they are small), comb their hair, and if necessary, change their clothes. They are little treasures and he would like to see them playing the part.

Minimize all noise. At the time of his arrival, eliminate all noise of the washer, dryer, dishwasher, or vacuum. Try to encourage the children to be quiet.

Be happy to see him. Greet him with a warm smile and be glad to see him.

Some don'ts: Don't greet him with problems and complaints. Don't complain if he is late for dinner. Count this as minor compared to what he might have gone through that day.

Make him comfortable. Have him lean back in a comfortable chair or suggest that he lie down in the bedroom. Have a cool or warm drink ready for him. Arrange his pillow and offer to take off his shoes. Speak in a low, soft, soothing and pleasant voice. Allow him to relax and unwind.

Listen to him. You may have a dozen things to tell him, but the moment of his arrival is not the time. Let him talk first.

Make the evening his. Never complain if he does not take you out to dinner or to other pleasant entertainment. Instead, try to understand his world of strain and pressure, his need to unwind and relax.

The goal: Try to make your home a place of peace and order where your husband can relax in body and spirit.

Changing Times

What is the role of the father in a family?

What is the role of the mother in a family?

Should both parents work outside the home when children are small? If not, who should stay home?

How has the women's movement improved society?

How has the women's movement hurt society?

Where do you see yourself in fifteen or twenty years in relation to career and family?

Are men better suited for the leadership of companies, institutions, and government? Why or why not?

Are jobs that are usually held by women (such as teacher, nurse, child care worker, social worker, and lay minister) as valuable as jobs more typically held by men (such as accountant, construction worker, computer scientist, and engineer)? How do you think the wages for those jobs compare?

How do you feel about affirmative action, with regard to gender, in the workplace? In other words, should women be given preference for jobs that have typically been held by men?

How do you feel about affirmative action, with regard to gender, in schools? Should specialty schools such as law schools and medical schools make sure they have male and female students in equal numbers?

Do you think that women who are elected to public office make decisions differently than men? Explain.

Do you think that God intended certain roles for men and women? Give a reason for your answer.

Does a sexist world hurt men as well as women? Why or why not?

That Was Then

Blessed art Thou, O Lord . . . for not creating me a woman. (Morning prayer of Orthodox Jewish men)

The whole education of women should be relative to men. To please them, to be useful to them, to win their love and esteem, to bring them up when young, to tend them when grown, to advise and console them; these are the duties of women at all times, and what they ought to learn from infancy. (Jean-Jacques Rousseau, 1712–1778)

Women are the gates of hell. (Saint Jerome, about 347–420)

As regards the individual nature, woman is defective and misbegotten. (Saint Thomas Aquinas, about 1224–1274)

A woman should be covered with shame at the thought that she is a woman. (Saint Clement of Alexandria, about 150–215)

The only useless life is woman's. (Benjamin Disraeli, 1804–1881)

Women are nothing but machines for producing children. (Napoléon Bonaparte, 1769–1821)

Sensible and responsible women do not want to vote. (Grover Cleveland, 1837–1908)

In childhood a woman must be subject to her father; in youth, to her husband; when her husband is dead, to her sons. A woman must never be free of subjugation. (Hindu Code of Manu)

Woman is something deficient or accidental. For the active power of the male intends to produce a perfect likeness of itself with male sex. If a female is conceived, this is due to lack of strength in the active power, to a defect in the mother, or to some external influence like that of a humid wind from the south. (Saint Thomas Aquinas, about 1224–1274)

Among all savage beasts none is found so harmful as woman. (Saint John Chrysostom, about 347–407)

Women are not made to the image of God. I feel nothing so casts down the manly mind from its heights as the fondling of woman and those bodily contacts that belong to the married state. (Saint Augustine of Hippo, 354–430)

Do you not know that you are Eve? . . . You are the devil's gateway. . . . How easily you destroyed man, the image of God. Because of the death which you brought upon us, even the Son of God had to die. (Tertullian, about 155–after 220)

To be slow in words is a woman's only virtue. (William Shakespeare, 1564–1616)

According to the Bible, woman was the last thing God made. It must have been a Saturday night. Clearly, he was tired. (Alexandre Dumas, 1802–1870)

Woman is slow in understanding and her unstable and naive mind renders her by way of natural weakness to the necessity of a strong hand in her husband. Her "use" is two-fold: animal sex and motherhood. (Saint Gregory the Great, about 540–604)

Do not be content merely to accept, and—one might say—to tolerate this authority of your husband, to whom God has subjected you according to the dispositions of nature and grace; in your sincere submission you must love that authority. . . . Many voices will suggest rather a proud autonomy; they will repeat that you are in every respect the equal of your husband. . . . Do not react like Eve to these lying, tempting, deceitful voices. (Pope Pius XII, 1876–1958)

This Is Now

At present women are taking their places in almost all professions and cultural, social and political institutions as well as in international organizations. Like others, the Catholic woman plays her part in these movements. She cannot and must not evade them. (Pope Pius XII, 1957)

Man and woman are in the image of God, equal in dignity and possessing the same rights. (Pope Pius XII, 1957)

When it is recognized that woman as a person possesses the power to communicate, to integrate, to bring to life, to heal, and to sensitize, a forward step will have been taken toward total humanization of culture. (Bishop Carroll T. Dozier, 1975)

Since women are becoming ever more conscious of their human dignity, they will not tolerate being treated as mere material instruments, but demand rights befitting a human person both in domestic and public life. (Pope John XXIII, 1963)

Where they have not yet won it, women claim for themselves an equality before the law and in fact. (Vatican Council II, 1965)

With respect to the fundamental rights of the person, every type of discrimination, whether social or cultural, whether based on sex, race, color, social condition, language, or religion, is to be overcome and eradicated as contrary to God's intent. (Vatican Council II, 1965)

Like the universal movements for peace, for amnesty, for justice; the woman's movement is international. Its influence can be a significant factor in the universal proclamation of the Word of God. (Bishop Carroll T. Dozier, 1975)

In the future, women will contribute to culture in ways that are both traditional and new. . . . We follow a Lord who makes all things new, and we can hope that men and women of the future will live in a culture transformed by feminine consciousness and nurturance. The coming of full equality of women can be a revolution that will increase joy, justice, and peace. Then, all manner of things will be well. (U.S. Bishops' Committee on Women in Society and in the Church, 1991)

We are very good at waiting. As women, we have waited for centuries. . . . We have been waiting, with Mary Magdalene, since Christ's death and resurrection, for our words of wisdom to not only be heard but to be believed. (Diana Hayes, 1991)

Women have a full right to become actively involved in all areas of public life, and this right must be affirmed and guaranteed. (Pope John Paul II, 1994)

I make an appeal to the women of the church today to assume new forms of leadership in service, and I appeal to all the institutions of the church to welcome this contribution of women. (Pope John Paul II, 1995)

We can say with certainty that discrimination against women contradicts the will of Christ. We are painfully aware that sexism, defined as "unjust discrimination based on sex," is still present in some members of the church. We reject sexism and pledge renewed efforts to guard against it in church teaching and practice. (U.S. Bishops, 1994)

All people are created in God's image, and each one is a reflection of goodness and grace. I embrace the church's vision of the human person that every man, woman and child possesses dignity and worth, and from our very conception we are ordered by God and "destined for eternal beatitude." (Archbishop Alex Brunett, 2000, paraphrasing *Catechism of the Catholic Church,* number 1711)

As archbishop, I apologize for those times and occasions when church leaders, male or female, have demeaned and devalued the invaluable role of women in the church or even their precious presence. (Archbishop Alex Brunett, 2000)

The education and empowerment of women throughout the world cannot fail to result in a more caring, tolerant and peaceful life for all. (Aung San Suu Kyi, winner of the 1991 Nobel Peace Prize)

The drive for women's equality, freedom and dignity in the last two centuries is not just a secular political movement, but a profoundly moral and spiritual quest not only for women but for men too, for the whole of human society. (Patricia McGuire, 2000)

To the young women of the church, we say: Carry forward the cause of gospel feminism. We will be with you along the way, sharing what we have learned about the freedom, joy and power of contemplative intimacy with God. We ask you to join us in a commitment to far-reaching transformation of church and society in non-violent ways. (Madeleva Manifesto, 2000)

Inclusive Language Is Gender Fair

With your partner, rework each of the following words, phrases, and sentences to include both men and women, while remaining true to its original meaning. Write each new statement under the old one.

the common man

fireman

family of man

chairman

man and wife

policeman

forefathers

congressman

man's search for meaning

spokesman

Good News for mankind

pilgrim fathers

Kingdom of God

my brother's keeper

sons of God

man overboard

What God has joined, man must not divide.

Peace on earth; goodwill to men.

Hey, you guys.

girls in the office

manpower

God, our Father

workman's compensation

Jesus came to save all men.

No man is an island.

brethren

everything known to man

Thou shalt not covet thy neighbor's wife.

God became man.

Media Messages

Challenging the Culture of Media

Springboard Activity

Magazine Models and Messages

This activity is designed to raise the girls' consciousness of how women are portrayed in the media, especially in magazine advertising. In contrast to the culture's tendency to objectify women and use sex to sell, our faith reminds us that God has made women in the divine image and calls them to fulfill that image.

Some girls may comment that you are exaggerating the issue or stretching to find examples. If so, acknowledge their feelings while pointing out that though advertisers may not intentionally set out to degrade women, negative images do have a toxic effect.

This activity can be done effectively with girls in middle school and high school.

Preparation
○ Read the background information near the end of this theme, and gather and review a few magazines that appeal to teenage girls (like *Seventeen, YM,* and *Teen Vogue*).
○ Ask the girls to bring in recent issues of their favorite magazines that they are willing to cut up.
○ Cut three different teen magazine covers into approximately equal numbers of pieces, together totaling the number of girls in your group.
○ Write each of the following headings on the top of a separate piece of newsprint:
  • Advertising that features just women
  • Advertising that features men and women together
  • Headlines of articles, stories, and features
○ Cut out teen magazine ads that blatantly use sex to sell things. (Save one of those ads for the additional activity "Active Advertising Acknowledgment.")

1. Focus the girls on the topic by asking questions like the ones that follow:

◉ How many of you subscribe to a teen magazine?

◉ What are your favorite magazines for teen girls?

◉ Can you name any magazines for teen boys? How are they different from those aimed at girls?

◉ What appeals to you or attracts you most when you look at magazines?

◉ What don't you like about typical teen magazines?

2. Offer the following comments in your own words:

◉ *Exploitation* means "the use of something or someone selfishly for one's own advantage." When companies exploit the gift of sexuality, they suggest that women, or less frequently men, are objects or playthings. Sometimes, that practice is known as sexploitation. Many companies use sex appeal to promote products. Sometimes they do this through ads that are overtly sexual. More often, the message is more subtle, and we may not even be aware of it.

Ask the group to name commercials, billboards, ads on buses or trains, and other types of advertisements that use sex to sell something. Announce that in this activity, the group will be analyzing media messages in magazines for sexploitation.

3. Distribute the puzzle pieces you cut from magazine covers and make cellophane tape available. Instruct the girls to form groups with those who have pieces from the same covers and to reconstruct their covers using the tape.

4. When the groups have formed, give each one some used magazines, scissors, glue or tape, and one of the newsprint sheets you labeled. Explain that each group is to look through the magazines, cut out items that illustrate the heading on the newsprint, and glue or tape the items onto the newsprint.

Allow 10 to 15 minutes for this task. As the groups finish, hang their sheets of newsprint where everyone can see them.

5. Gather the girls in front of the newsprint sheets to examine, analyze, and discuss common themes or images among the examples. Encourage them to articulate their insights, and point out things you notice in their examples. Also show the ads you cut out that illustrate sexploitation of women, and point out details in those ads.

6. Invite the girls to discuss questions like these:

◉ Are these advertisements successful in promoting their products?

◉ Do they make you want to buy their products or read the magazines' articles?

◉ How many of the magazines we used today feature boys on the cover? girls?

◉ What serious subjects are highlighted on the covers?

◉ What issues would you like to see covered in magazines?

7. Close the activity by challenging the girls to look carefully at the magazines they read and, in particular, at how advertising in those magazines exploits girls and women. Suggest that when they find an ad that is offensive, they write a letter of protest to the magazine publisher and the company that makes the product being advertised.

Additional Activities

Just the Facts

This forced choice activity presents some surprising facts and issues to raise the girls' awareness of the impact of media. It can be done with girls in middle school and high school.

Preparation
○ Create two signs for the room, "True" and "False." Post the signs on opposite walls.

Read the following statements. After each one, ask the girls to decide whether it is true or false and to move to the side of the room that indicates their response. When everyone has made their move, read the corresponding fact and invite discussion.

Statements	*Facts*
◈ The average American sees about three hundred advertisements a day.	False. The number is about three thousand ads a day, on television, radio, billboards, Internet sites, newspapers, buses, taxis, storefronts, magazines, and clothes, and at entertainment venues, especially movie theaters and sports facilities (Jean Kilbourne, *Deadly Persuasion,* p. 58).
◈ Girls' magazines lead to body image problems among young women.	True. About 70 percent of girls in fifth through twelfth grades say magazine pictures influence their idea of the perfect body shape (Atlanta Anti-Eating Disorders League). The same percentage of college women say they feel worse about their own looks after reading women's magazines (Kilbourne, p. 133).
◈ Being concerned about their appearance is natural for all adolescents.	True. However, a study of both men and women found that a preoccupation with one's appearance takes a toll on mental health, including diminished mental performance, increased feelings of shame and anxiety, depression,

sexual dysfunction, and the development of eating disorders (Kilbourne, p. 133).

◉ Magazine ads give girls conflicting messages about who they should be.

True. The culture suggests that both men and women must work hard and produce and achieve success, and yet, at the same time, encourages them to live impulsively and to spend a lot of money pursuing immediate gratification. Additionally, girls are expected to be sexual but innocent, to be nice but strong.

◉ We cannot do anything about the effects of advertising.

False. Becoming more aware of the effects of all kinds of media can help us to be more enlightened consumers and to critique the culture in which we live. Additionally, we can take active roles in boycotting products that demean girls and women, promote irresponsible sexual attitudes, and suggest that violence is acceptable. We can also write to companies, legislators, newspapers, and magazines and voice our dissatisfaction. Girls are a powerful consumer group and can make a difference by changing attitudes.

Active Advertising Acknowledgment

This activity gives the girls a series of questions to help them determine whether an ad exploits girls or women. It is most appropriate for high school girls. However, young adolescent girls can benefit from the process if carefully led by an adult.

Preparation
○ Write the following statements on newsprint or the board:
- Become more *active*.
- Pay attention to the *advertising* messages that bombard you daily.
- *Acknowledge* their impact on you.

1. Read the statements you posted on the board, and show the girls one of the sexploitation ads that you cut out for the springboard activity. Distribute handout 5, "Active Advertising Acknowledgment," and encourage the girls to complete it individually, using that ad.

2. When everyone has finished the handout, ask them to share their answers with one or two other people, noting how the advertisement might affect people differently. After a few minutes, invite the girls to share their insights or comments with everyone.

3. If time permits, repeat this exercise with another advertisement. Or make magazines available and invite the girls to find their own ads to use in actively acknowledging the impact of advertising.

Images of Media Women

This activity focuses on women in television, but it can easily be adapted to focus on movie celebrities or pop music stars. It can be used with high school girls as is, or with middle school girls if more direct guidance is provided, especially in step 3.

1. Ask the girls to name their favorite female characters (not actresses) in popular television series. List their responses on newsprint or the board.

2. Pose questions like these:
◎ What qualities make these characters popular?
◎ How ethnically or racially diverse is the list?
◎ How many of these characters have a principal role in their series?
◎ Do you know anything about the families (such as mothers, fathers, and children) of these characters?
◎ Do you know anything about the religions or faiths of these characters?
◎ What are their professions?
◎ How important is beauty to their success? How important is thinness or body type?

3. Divide the girls into small groups and assign each group two or three characters from the list. Give everyone handout 6, "Evaluating Women in the Media," and direct the groups each to compare the behaviors of their assigned characters with the behaviors listed on the handout. (If you prefer, instead of distributing the handout, simply copy the lists from it onto newsprint or the board.)

4. When the groups have completed their comparison, gather them and discuss their findings. Close the activity by comparing the behavior and characteristics of media women with those of women who are part of the girls' lives every day.

(This activity is adapted from Center for Media Literacy, *Break the Lies that Bind,* p. 28.)

Music Media

This activity encourages critical assessment of the music that is pervasive in the life of most teens. It is appropriate for all teens.

Preparation

○ Ask the girls to bring compact discs and tapes, with liner notes that contain lyrics. Suggest that they bring samples of different genres of music.

1. Gather the recordings and create small groups using the genres of music represented—for example, gospel might be one group, rock another, and rap another. Give the appropriate recordings and lyrics to each group. Tell the groups to read the lyrics and analyze them for messages by and about women. Suggest that they focus on questions such as these:

◎ What percentage of the artists assigned to your group are women?

◎ How are women represented in the lyrics you received?

◎ How important are the lyrics to the songs? Do most people listen to the lyrics?

◎ What kinds of messages about women are conveyed in the songs? Give specific examples. Are women longing for love? Are women the objects of love?

◎ Are there any sexual themes in the songs?

◎ Are any of the lyrics violent? If so, is the violence directed at women or committed by women?

2. Ask each group to select two songs—one illustrating negative attitudes about women, the other illustrating positive attitudes—and play them for everyone. Invite a representative from each group to explain how the group critiqued and chose each song.

3. Conclude this activity by asking for general insights and comments about women as musicians and as the subjects of songs.

Monitoring the News

This activity leads the girls through a gender survey of their local newspaper, for clues about how women are represented in and to their community. It is most appropriate for high school girls, though mature middle school girls will benefit from it. It can be done individually or as a group.

1. Make available copies of the local newspaper, or ask the girls to bring copies. Provide four colors of highlighters and offer these directions:

◎ Go through the paper and highlight male bylines (author lines) with one color, female bylines a second color, male newsmakers (subjects of articles or photos) a third color, and female newsmakers a fourth color.

Direct the girls to do the same analysis for several issues of the paper. Then instruct them to find the total number of people they highlighted in each category and figure out the percentages of female authors and female subjects.

2. Follow up your monitoring project with a strategy session to help the girls find ways to publicize their findings, including discussing them with the paper's editor or stockholders. Consider doing a similar study of school newspapers, weekly newsmagazines, or other local publications.

(This activity is adapted from the Center for Media and Values, "How to Conduct a Gender Study of Your Local Newspaper.")

Pornography: The Ultimate Sexism

Though middle school girls may be well aware of pornography, this activity may be a little too much for them. It is most appropriate for girls in high school.

1. Write the following quote on newsprint or the board: "Sex in advertising is pornographic because it dehumanizes and objectifies people, especially women" (Jean Kilbourne, *Deadly Persuasion,* p. 271). Discuss the statement, using questions like these:

- According to this definition, how much of advertising could be considered pornographic?
- How does it feel to watch sexual scenes on television or in movies, with a date?
- How does pornography hurt women physically, emotionally, and spiritually? How does it hurt men?

2. Close by affirming the right belief that all people possess human dignity and anything that objectifies a person is ultimately sinful.

Options and Actions

- Over the course of a few weeks, have the girls create a scrapbook or portfolio of advertisements. Ask that they include comments about why each ad is offensive or how it promotes healthy images of girls and women. Invite everyone to present their work to the group.
- Suggest that the girls keep a journal for one particular form of the media: music, music videos, television, movies, magazines, or whatever. Instruct them to record examples that they find particularly offensive, and examples that present healthy attitudes toward women. Assign each person a partner with whom to compare notes periodically.
- Arrange to take the girls to a local mall or shopping area. Before you head out, divide them into pairs, distribute pencils and paper, and instruct the pairs to count how many advertisements they encounter in a defined time period, starting as soon as you leave your meeting space. Tell them to include advertisements on vehicles, billboards, flyers on telephone poles, commercials on the radio, messages on T-shirts, and so on. Afterward, tally everyone's results and calculate the hourly average of advertisements encountered per person.
- Have the girls each create their own advertisement that conveys a healthy message about girls and women. The advertisement can be in any media form: magazine, billboard, video, audio, or whatever.
- Invite mothers and mentors to a session about women in the media. Compare women's magazines with teen magazines. Discuss how the media have changed in

the last generation, asking, "Who were the women role models for your mothers and mentors?" Consider showing an *I Love Lucy* episode as a starter for a discussion on how women's roles in television and in the culture have changed since the 1950s.

- Organize a boycott of products that use offensive advertising, or a "buycott" of products that use female-positive advertising. Make this a school- or parishwide campaign, educating others about the reason for the boycott or buycott.
- Check out advertisements in magazines intended for children and on children's television programs. Discuss the messages children receive from those media.
- Instruct the girls to review music videos at home and to take notes about how the males and females in them are dressed, how they behave, how they relate with one another, how the females are presented, and what role violence plays. You might suggest that they tape representative parts of the broadcasts to present to the group. Help them share and discuss their findings. Close by challenging them to think critically about the portrayal of women in music videos, which are generally crafted to appeal to young men. (This activity is adapted from Myra Junyk, "Using Rock Videos to Analyze MTV.")

Reflection and Discussion

Journal Questions

- ⊚ Media nutrition is like food nutrition: it depends on what we ingest, in what form, and in what amount. Write a personal media nutrition plan and explain how it may hurt or harm your spirit—the essence of who you are.
- ⊚ For one week, list all the television shows, radio stations, magazines, and Internet sites that are part of your life. At the end of the week, analyze your list. Which media sources are good for your spirit? Which sources should you limit or eliminate?
- ⊚ Who are your media role models? What qualities do they possess that you admire? Which of those qualities can help you grow into the fullness of life that God intended for you?
- ⊚ Write a letter to an imaginary girl who is seven to ten years younger than you. Tell her what you have learned about the impact and the messages of media on girls. Suggest ways that she can make herself media smart, that is, resistant to negative media messages.

Scriptural Connections

- Prov. 1:7–10 (Do not be enticed by sinners.)
- Matt. 13:24–30 (The parable of the wheat and the weeds)
- 2 Cor. 5:1–5 (We must take care of our earthly "tent.")
- Second John (False messages of deceivers)

WomanWisdom Quotes

[On television, you just never see] women of color and Jewish women and . . . Asian women. . . . I think that's very damaging to little girls' sense of self-esteem. (Roseanne Arnold)

All our advertising is propaganda, of course, but it has become so much a part of our life, is so pervasive, that we just don't know what it is propaganda *for*. (Pauline Kael)

The tragedy of our time is not that we are so eye centered, so appearance besotted. The tragedy is that we do not know what we like until we are told by our advertisers and entertainers. (Jessamyn West)

The thief comes only to steal and kill and destroy. I came that they may have life, and have it abundantly. (Jesus, in John 10:10)

Prayer

As I am growing up I see,
    So many things a girl should be.
    We should be paper thin,
    We must have the clearest skin.
    We must look like a perfect model.
    We must have that hair color,
    Even if it is out of a bottle.
    We must have the most fashionable clothes,
    And the coolest car if we drove.
    We must have the best hairstyle,
    Even though we know it will change in a while.

All these things a girl is supposed to be,
When all I really want to be is me.
    I don't need to be paper thin,
    Or have the clearest skin.
    I don't want to look like a skinny model,
    Rather a healthy sports player.
    I don't want that bottled color hair,
    I would rather have people stare at my natural hair.
    I don't want the fashionable clothes that will make me moan and groan,
    I would rather wear something I could bear to stay in.
    And when I drive I don't want the coolest car,
    Just one that will let me go far.
    I don't want the best hairstyle,
    Because I know that it will change in a while.
    I would rather have a hairstyle, that I would want to live with for a while.

All these things we are pressured to be.
So please, dear God, help me to realize
That to be just like YOU,
Is the coolest thing that I could ever do. Amen.

(Amanda Marie Magnan, "Please Help Me to Be Myself")

Resource Materials

Print

Kilbourne, Jean. *Deadly Persuasion: Why Women and Girls Must Fight the Addictive Power of Advertising.* New York: Free Press, 1999. This book focuses on girls and women who are at special risk in a toxic cultural environment.

Maine, Margo. *Body Wars: Making Peace with Women's Bodies.* Carlsbad, CA: Gürze Books, 2000. The chapter on advertising in this book provides interesting facts about the media culture, strategies for change, guidelines for letter writing, and addresses of major networks. Other chapters include information on body image, weight-ism, and violence against women. Aimed at adult women, this easy-to-read work offers much wisdom for adolescent girls.

Video

Dreamworlds (Foundation for Media Education, 1990, 55 minutes) and *Dreamworlds Two* (Media Education Foundation, 1995, 57 minutes). These documentaries combine powerful imagery from over two hundred videos, with narrative on the impact of sexual imagery in music videos. They are available through Media Education Foundation, 26 Center Street, Northampton, MA 01060; 800-897-0089; *www.mediaed.org.*

Killing Us Softly Three. Media Education Foundation. 2000. 34 minutes. This video, by Jean Kilbourne, is available through Media Education Foundation.

Internet

www.about-face.org. About-Face. Devoted to healthy body images, this site features pictures of the Top 10 offensive ads for women, each with commentary and analysis.

www.medialit.org. Center for Media Literacy. This site and its sponsoring organization provide multiple resources for adults concerned with the influence of advertising, violence, and other media elements. The resources may be reviewed and purchased at the Web site.

Background Information

We live in a media culture. Every aspect of our life is influenced by what we see and hear in television, movies, radio, books, newspapers, magazines, sound recordings, billboards, the Internet, junk mail, and so on. Imagine what life would be like without that constant bombardment. Like we seldom notice how the air that we breathe affects our body, we rarely are conscious of how the media influence us as individuals or as a society.

Because God created us to be in harmony with the world and with one another, and ultimately, with the divine Creator, it is crucial that we learn to be conscious of media messages that may be dangerous to our integrity as persons.

In our media culture, women and girls are particularly susceptible to dangerous images that keep them from being who God created them to be. The media often portray them as objects of beauty whose bodies are sexual and whose voices are silent or unimportant.

By looking critically at just one form of media—girls' and women's magazines— we can become more aware of how females are often exploited in the media in general. Throughout history, women have been relegated to roles that emphasize beauty and romantic relationships. Today's media compound that problem with a pervasive culture of sexploitation, which contributes to the difficulties of adolescent girls. Though the media do not directly cause eating disorders, loss of self-esteem, and promiscuous sexual activity, studies indicate that they are a factor.

Jean Kilbourne, in her book *Deadly Persuasion,* reports that the average American is exposed to over three thousand advertisements a day (p. 58). A constant barrage of product advertisements promise happiness and success. However, in reality, mass media overload often leads to the opposite, particularly for teenage girls. Today's female teens are engaging in far riskier health behavior in greater numbers than have females of any prior teen generation (p. 129). "The culture, both reflected and rein-forced by advertising, urges girls to adopt a false self, to bury alive their real selves, to become 'feminine,' which means to be nice and kind and sweet, to compete with other girls for the attention of boys, and to value romantic relationships with boys above all else" (p. 130).

Becoming media literate is crucial to the emotional and spiritual well-being of girls. Though it is not possible to remove oneself from the culture, it *is* possible to become more aware of marketing techniques that are exploitive. And learning to recognize the influence of advertising can help lessen its negative impact.

Some common examples of negative advertising techniques are these:

- The models look too thin, are partially clothed, or are posed in sexual positions such as with their breasts as the focal point or with their legs apart.
- The actual products do not occupy a significant part of the ad, but may be strategi-cally placed so that they become part of a sexual message.
- A focus on only certain parts of a model's body, such as the legs, suggests dismem-berment and the insignificance of face and voice.
- Facial expressions emphasize sexuality. Smiles are less common than sensual pouts. Mouths may be open provocatively.

- When men and women are in the same scene, men often occupy dominant positions, looking at the camera, while the women are in subservient positions, looking up at the men.
- Young adolescent girls may be used to convey the sexual appeal of innocence.
- When a man is photographed with more than one woman, it conveys the message that women are in competition for male attention.
- Frequently, scenes suggest violence against women. Sometimes, the violence may look like just rough play, since the woman is smiling or appears to be going along.

Sexist themes that suggest women are weaker and less intelligent while emphasizing boys and men in strong leadership roles are prevalent in both the advertising and the articles of women's magazines. Common themes on the covers of magazines are beauty, fashion, and ways to attract and keep males.

It is common to deny that advertising influences us or that advertisers deliberately deceive or exploit. However, it is important to recognize that companies pay thousands, sometimes millions, for advertising. Photographic details are intentional and carefully planned to influence consumers. Advertisers use the medium of teen magazines because they know that adolescent girls have tremendous buying power.

It is also important to note that the church does not believe that sex itself is bad, though it does hold that using sex to sell is a violation of the beauty and goodness of God's gift of sexuality. Pierre Teilhard de Chardin said that *"nothing . . . is profane* for those who know how to see" (*The Divine Milieu,* p. 35). Learning to "see" beyond the superficial images of the media reinforces the right belief in the goodness of every human being, who is a reflection of God.

Notes

Use this space to jot ideas, reminders, and additional resources.

Active Advertising Acknowledgment

Consider the ad provided by your leader, and answer the following questions:

What product is this ad promoting?

What other messages and feelings are part of the ad?

How is the ad getting your attention, and how is it trying to convince you to buy the product?

Are the people in the ad realistically depicted?

How diverse are the people in the ad?

What do you like about the ad?

What don't you like about the ad?

Will the ad influence your decision to buy the product?

What would you change in the ad if you were in charge?

(The questions on this handout are adapted from Margo Maine, PhD, *Body Wars: Making Peace with Women's Bodies* [Carlsbad, CA: Gürze Books, 2000], page 83. Copyright © 2000 by Margo Maine, PhD.)

Evaluating Women in the Media

Compare the behaviors of each character assigned to your group with the behaviors listed below.

Traditional behaviors
○ works or acts under the direction of men
○ is emotionally expressive
○ is sensitive to others' feelings
○ meets media standards of beauty
○ is seen primarily as a sex object
○ works with others
○ provides emotional support for men
○ engages in home-related activities

Nontraditional behaviors
○ takes risks and acts independently
○ is brusque and aggressive
○ thinks rather than feels
○ has an unconventional or unimportant appearance
○ has nonsexual and nonmarital friendships with men
○ is a loner
○ takes charge of situations
○ thinks logically
○ is a professional or business leader

(Adapted from Center for Media Literacy, *Break the Lies that Bind: Sexism in the Media* [Los Angeles: Center for Media Literacy, 1994], page 28. Copyright © 1990 by the Center for Media Literacy.)

Standing Up for Yourself

Challenging the Culture of Violence

The activities in this theme challenge the girls to examine violence against women along a continuum from sexual harassment to rape. Raising the consciousness of girls to enable them to recognize subtle and overt forms of violence empowers them to prevent, challenge, and report behaviors that are harmful.

The strategies in this theme focus on three main areas of violence:

* sexual harassment in the adolescent culture
* verbal and physical abuse in teen relationships
* acquaintance rape

The activities are most appropriate for high school girls, but they can be effective with younger teens when handled in an age-appropriate way and with sufficient help from adult leaders.

Springboard Activities

Recognizing and Naming Sexual Harassment

Preparation

○ Post the following definition of sexual harassment: "Sexual advances, requests for sexual favors, verbal comments, or physical contact that is deemed uncomfortable or unwelcome by the person on the receiving end."

○ You might want to copy each role-play scenario from step 5 onto a separate index card or slip of paper.

1. Read the definition of sexual harassment that you posted. Divide the girls into two equal groups and give each group newsprint and markers. Ask the groups to brainstorm behaviors and comments that they think fit the definition. Caution them to avoid telling stories at this point—to just list the behaviors in short phrases. Allow 5 to 10 minutes for this brainstorming.

2. Post the groups' lists and discuss similarities between them. Then compare the items on the girls' lists with the following behaviors reported in U.S. high schools, and point out any similarities or differences.

touching (arm, breast, buttock, and so on)
making verbal comments (about parts of the body, sex, clothing, looks, and so on)
calling names (including terms like honey, babe, and worse)
spreading sexual rumors
leering and staring
sharing sexual or "dirty" jokes and cartoons
showing lewd pictures and pornography
leaving sexual messages or graffiti on computers, or playing sexually offensive
    computer games
gesturing with the hands or body
pressuring for sexual activity
cornering, blocking, standing too close, and following
having conversations that are too personal
"rating" an individual—for example, on a scale from 1 to 10
wearing obscene T-shirts, hats, and pins
showing R-rated movies
committing sexual assault or attempted sexual assault
committing rape
massaging the neck or shoulders
touching oneself sexually in front of others
drawing graffiti
making kissing sounds; licking the lips suggestively
repeatedly asking someone out when he or she is not interested
"spiking" (pulling down someone's pants)
making suggestive facial expressions (winking, kissing, and so on)
passing "slam books" (lists of students' names with derogatory sexual comments
written by other students)
making out in the hallway

3. Point out that sexual harassment is not the same as flirting, which is commonly accepted as reasonably harmless in our culture. Clarify the difference by asking questions such as the ones that follow:

◎ What is the major difference between sexual harassment and flirting? [Flirting feels good to both parties involved. Sexual harassment does not feel good to the person who is being harassed.]

◎ Can flirting turn into sexual harassment? If so, how? [Yes. The person being flirted with might pretend to go along when she really does not like it. Or she might not mind it at first but stops feeling good about it, and the other person keeps doing it anyway.]

Use points like these to emphasize that what matters is how the person on the receiving end perceives the behavior:

◉ Sexual harassment in schools and in the workplace is illegal. The law is concerned with the effect of the behavior, not the intent of the behavior. In other words, the law is concerned with how the person on the receiving end is affected by the behavior, not with what the person on the giving end means by the behavior.

◉ Sexual harassment is always wrong in any setting, whether or not it qualifies as illegal. It is wrong to do or say anything that we know could hurt another person, and it is important to consider and respect others' feelings.

◉ Sexual harassment is also contrary to the intention and will of God because it hurts another human being and reduces the gift of sexuality to a power used over another person. It is contrary to the Gospel vision of full humanity for all persons and right relations among all creatures.

4. Ask the girls to return to their groups, and give each group another sheet of newsprint. Explain that one group is to list how a girl feels when she is being flirted with. The other group should list feelings associated with sexual harassment. Have the groups post and compare their completed lists.

5. Invite the girls to practice recognizing the difference between a compliment and sexual harassment by observing and participating in spontaneous role-plays. Ask for volunteers to play a variety of characters, and assign them scenarios from the following list:

- *Example role-play 1 (one boy, one girl).* Boy says to girl, "Gee, you look great in that sweater today"; girl, taking it as a compliment, says, "Thank you."
- *Example role-play 2 (one boy, one girl).* Boy rolls his eyes, winks, makes rude gestures with his hands, and says to girl, "He-e-e-ey . . . you look GREAT in that sweater today!"; girl, flustered, walks away.
- *Role-play 1 (one boy, one girl).* Boy chases girl, begging for a hug, grabs her, and buries his head in her chest.
- *Role-play 2 (one male teacher, group of girls).* Teacher approaches girls and teases one of them about a button missing from her blouse.
- *Role-play 3 (group of girls, one boy).* Girls taunt boy about his small stature and the possible size of his genitals.
- *Role-play 4 (group of boys, two girls).* Boys make comments about girls' appearance, rating them on a scale of 1 to 10.
- *Role-play 5 (two girls, one male teacher).* Girls come into coed physical education class late, and teacher tells them to do twenty jumping jacks in front of the class.
- *Role-play 6 (one boy, one girl).* Boy blocks a door and tells girl if she wants to come in, she will have to give him a kiss.

Call the volunteers who receive the example role-plays to act them out, in order, before the group. Then offer the following explanation in your own words:

◉ The first example is not sexual harassment. The boy intends his statement as a compliment, and the girl takes it that way. In the second example, however, the boy's body language, gestures, and tone of voice make a big difference, and the girl may feel angry, embarrassed, or even guilty. The second example is sexual harassment.

Give the other volunteers time to prepare their scenarios, and then invite them to share their role-plays with the rest of the group. After each scenario is presented, discuss questions like the ones that follow:

◉ Is this sexual harassment?

◉ Who is the victim or victims; who is the harasser or harassers?

◉ What can and should be done about the incident?

(This activity is adapted from Susan Strauss with Pamela Espeland, *Sexual Harassment and Teens,* pp. 44–47 and 107–108.)

Verbal Abuse and Physical Violence

Preparation

○ Create a violence continuum by posting signs with the following labels across the length of a wall:

• Nonviolent

• Slightly violent

• Violent

• Very violent

1. Define *violence* as "harming or destroying the well-being or existence of a person, group, or community" (Julia Ahlers and Michael Wilt, *Christian Justice,* p. 101). Define *domestic violence* as "battering, emotional and psychological abuse, or sexual assault that attempts to control a person through fear and intimidation in their own home" (adapted from p. 195). Ask the girls if they would make any changes to those definitions.

2. Point out the continuum on the wall and tell the girls that you will read a series of situations. Explain that after you read each situation, they are to move to the point along the continuum that they feel represents the level of violence achieved by the action. Then read the following statements, allowing time for reaction, discussion, and comments after each one:

◉ A teacher calls a student stupid and lazy.

◉ A parent slaps a child for talking back.

◉ Someone makes fun of another person, humiliating him.

◉ A guy tells a girl that she is fat.

◉ A girl tells a guy that he is fat.

◉ A man tells his wife that she can't do anything right.

◉ A guy pressures his girlfriend to see a movie that is pornographic.

◉ A boy uses physical force to kiss a girl against her wishes.

◉ Someone continues tickling a weaker person after she has asked the tickler to stop.

◉ A girl slaps a boy for making lewd comments about her or her clothing.

◉ A boy laces a girl's drink with alcohol or drugs without her knowledge.

3. Make the following points in your own words:

⊚ On average, each year between 1992 and 1996, about one million women and girls over age twelve experienced violence, including rape, sexual assault, robbery, and bodily assault, by a current or former boyfriend, partner, or husband (Margo Maine, *Body Wars,* p. 152).

⊚ Ninety-five percent of the victims of domestic violence in this country are women.

⊚ Physical abuse is often preceded or accompanied by verbal and emotional abuse.

4. Brainstorm advice for girls who think they are in abusive relationships. Then distribute and review handout 7, "Building Blocks in Understanding Teen Dating Violence."

Acquaintance Rape

1. Distribute handout 8, "Myths and Realities of Acquaintance Rape." Read each myth and its corresponding reality. Discuss any statements that generate controversy or disagreement.

2. Present the following facts about violence against women. You may want to write them on the board or transparencies or newsprint to make a visual impact. Discuss each fact, asking the participants if they are surprised by it or if they can offer any insights or opinions.

⊚ Seventy-eight women are raped each hour. (National Victim Center, 1992, in "Rape Facts II").

⊚ Sixty-one percent of all rapes occurred before the victim reached age eighteen. (National Women's Study, 1990, in "Rape Facts II").

⊚ A woman has a four-times greater chance of being raped by someone she knows than of being raped by a stranger. (Robin Warshaw, 1988, in "Date Rape").

⊚ Only 17 percent of rapists are strangers; 83 percent are acquaintances (friends of the family, dates, boyfriends, relatives, and authority figures). (Diana Russell, 1986, in "Date Rape"").

⊚ Fifty-five percent of stranger rapes are reported to the police; only 19 percent of acquaintance rapes are reported. (Diana Russell, 1986, in "Date Rape").

⊚ In one study, 83.5 percent of college men stated that "some women look like they are just asking to be raped" (Robin Warshaw and S. L. Books, 1988, in Margo Maine, *Body Wars,* p. 152).

3. Close this activity by eliciting from the group ideas about preventing acquaintance or date rape. Put those ideas on newsprint for future reference.

Additional Activities

Sexual Harassment: Assumptions and Attitudes

Preparation

○ Make a set of "assumptions and attitudes" cards with the following statements:
- She asked for it.
- She can't take a joke.
- All boys want is sex.
- The way she dresses, she wants it.
- Boys will be boys.
- It's only flirting.
- Everyone else does it.
- Let them have their fun.
- She's a troublemaker.
- She is a real prude.

Distribute the "assumptions and attitudes" cards randomly among the group. Explain that the word *assumption* means "a belief that is taken for granted or accepted as true, even if no real proof exists to support it." Ask those who are holding the cards to read their statements. After each statement, lead a discussion focused around questions such as these:

◉ What attitude does this statement indicate?

◉ How could this statement affect a victim of sexual harassment?

◉ How does this assumption and attitude affect efforts to live out the Gospel call to right relationship and deep and profound respect for all human beings?

(This activity is adapted from Susan Strauss with Pamela Espeland, *Sexual Harassment and Teens,* pp. 74 and 97.)

Reporting Sexual Harassment

Preparation

○ On a sheet of newsprint, mark off three equal sections. Label the sections as follows, and then post the newsprint where everyone can see it:
- It's about me.
- It's about others.
- It's about the system.
○ Bring in the sexual harassment policy from a local school or school district. If possible, provide a copy for each participant.

1. Create small groups of six to eight girls and distribute handout 9, "Why Victims Don't Report Sexual Harassment." Give a sheet of newsprint and a marker to each group and announce these instructions in your own words:

◉ Mark three equal spaces on your newsprint, as I did on the one that is posted. Then read the reasons listed on the handout, and record each one under the correct heading on the newsprint. Also add any other valid reasons that you think of.

2. When the small groups are done, gather them and compare lists. In your own words, deliver the following information and questions about the categories:

◉ *It's about me.* "Victims of sexual harassment and sexual assault tend to blame themselves. They actually believe that the harassment or assault happened because of something they said or did, or something they did not say or do. Either way, they see it as their fault. In fact, sexual harassment and assault are never, ever the victim's fault. They are the fault of the abuser" (adapted from Susan Strauss with Pamela Espeland, Sexual Harassment and Teens, p. 98).

◉ *It's about him.* "Sexual harassment keeps happening because people do not communicate clearly. For example, if a woman says no and smiles, a man may not believe that she means it. However, maybe she is smiling because she is embarrassed, or because she does not want to seem rude. Maybe she does not want to show her anger.

"Even if a woman says no without smiling, men may not believe that she means it. Boys are taught that when girls say no, they are just playing games or pretending, and they really mean maybe or yes. Girls are taught to put other people's feelings first. They do not want to hurt boys' feelings, so they are not honest about their own feelings" (adapted from p. 68).

However difficult, it is important that girls speak up. Most boys and men do not want to offend, and just letting them know how you feel can eliminate the offending behavior. If the behavior does not stop, or if speaking up leads to more disrespect, you need to seek the help of a trusted adult. Another option is to write a letter to the offender. In the letter, specify the behavior, how it makes you feel, and the fact that you want it stopped. Date the letter, give a copy to the harasser, give another copy to a trusted adult, and keep a copy for yourself.

◉ *It's about the system.* "[Distribute copies of a sexual harassment policy from a local school or school district.] Find the procedure for reporting incidents of sexual harassment. Does the procedure make it relatively easy for a victim to report an incident? Who are victims supposed to report to? Who are the people in your school that you would go to if you were being sexually harassed? Is this policy clear and usable? If not, what would you do to make it clearer or more accessible? [Follow through by taking the girls' suggestions to someone in the school administration or encouraging them to do so]" (adapted from pp. 99–100).

3. Distribute handout 10, "What to Do if It Happens to You." Discuss the steps listed on the handout, clarifying as necessary and naming trusted adults in the schools the girls attend.

Resisting Pressure

1. Introduce this activity using comments like these:
   ◉ When you love someone, you might be willing to give up something you feel is right in order to make that person happy. In a committed relationship, sacrifice and compromise can be beautiful, but sacrificing your principles, beliefs, and future for sex is a mistake.

   People sometimes use a line like, "If you love me, you'll prove it," to pressure a partner into having sex. When someone uses a line like that, it is important for the partner to resist the pressure both verbally and nonverbally. For instance, the partner might respond, "If you love me, you'll stop trying to make me do something I don't want to do" or "If you love me, you'll prove it by respecting my feelings."

2. Divide the group into pairs. Explain that the pairs are each to develop a 1-minute skit incorporating a pressure line and a response, with both partners taking an active role. Allow 15 to 20 minutes for the pairs to develop their skits and practice.

3. When they are ready, invite the girls to perform their skits for everyone. Discuss any issues and insights that arise during the presentations. Conclude this part of the activity with comments like these:
   ◉ If you have tried to clearly communicate your feelings and the other person does not get the message, stand up, back away, and with a serious or angry look, say: "I'm just not getting through to you—I don't want to have sex. You seem to care more about sex than you do about my feelings." Walk out. Get out of the situation so that you can think more clearly and the other person can cool down. Then you will not be as likely to be pressured into making a mistake.

4. Guide the group in brainstorming a list of do's and don'ts to help prevent acquaintance and date rape. Be sure to include alcohol and drugs in the don't list. Note that when someone is under the influence of alcohol or drugs, it is difficult for them to make good decisions or to make reasoned responses to pressure lines.

(This activity is adapted from Michael J. Basso, *The Underground Guide to Teenage Sexuality.*)

Options and Actions

- Tell some of the stories of biblical women who endured violence simply because they were women. Several of those stories are cited in the background information near the end of this theme.
- Recruit as guest speakers people who work with battered women and families, rape counselors, and advocates for women in harassment and abuse situations.
- Plan a prayer vigil in your school, parish, or community, for victims of sexual

violence and harassment. You might make the vigil part of National Women's History Month.

- Create a resource to distribute in your school or parish that includes thirty days of facts and statistics from this theme and related resources, and a prayer to be said each day.
- Plan a service opportunity at or for a shelter for battered women and families. Consider collecting supplies, raising money, or arranging special services.
- Assign individuals or small groups to research domestic violence and the resources your community offers its victims. Direct them to address questions like these:
  ○ Are there people within your diocese who advocate for women in difficult domestic situations?
  ○ Are there men's groups that address violence against women?
- Invite someone from a local college, university, school district, or diocesan office, who is familiar with policies about sexual harassment and acquaintance rape, to come and speak about prevention and reporting.
- Conduct a Bible study on violence and the Gospel response. Pay particular attention to Jesus' treatment of women and his words to people who harmed them.

Reflection and Discussion

Journal Questions

- ◉ Reflect on your own vulnerability as a girl. When and with whom do you feel safe? unsafe?
- ◉ In what ways does a culture that is violent toward girls and women also hurt boys and men?
- ◉ Where have you seen sexual harassment or violence in your own life? Write about an incident that involved you or someone you know well.
- ◉ Talk to a close male friend or relative about sexual harassment and violence from a male perspective. Write about any insights you gain.

Scriptural Connections

- Genesis, chapter 34 (the rape of Dinah)
- Ps. 31:10–15 (prayer of a person who endures pain)
- Matt. 5:3–11 (the Beatitudes)
- John 8:2–11 (the woman caught in adultery)
- 1 Cor. 5:9–13 (avoidance of sexually immoral persons)
- 1 Cor. 13:4–13 (the true meaning of love)

WomanWisdom Quotes

On the day when it will be possible for woman to love not in her weakness but in her strength, not to escape herself but to find herself, not to abase herself but to assert herself—on that day love will become for her, as for man, a source of life and not of mortal danger. (Simone de Beauvoir)

Bad judgment and carelessness are not punishable by rape. (Pearl Cleage)

We need to turn the question around to look at the harasser, not the target. We need to be sure that we can go out and look anyone who is a victim of harassment in the eye and say, "You do not have to remain silent anymore." (Anita Hill)

Prayer

Now I can see,
and I am no longer naïve.
The blinders have been taken away,
and I am free.
Yet I am trapped.
Trapped between good and evil,
between standing up and turning away.
For now I see the hate,
now I see your scorn.
I am no longer so blinded by innocence,
but aware by guilt.
Guilt for not stopping the bad,
the words, the punches, the knives.
Guilt for turning away,
for never believing things were bad.
But now I am old,
no longer naïve.
I see you and your hateful ways.
I see your scorn.
But through this I will be strong,
I will not succumb to the hate,
for I believe in good.
I will survive my journey,
with God by my side.
My journey from naïve baby,
my journey to find me.
(Seanne Casey, "Innocence Lost")

Resource Materials

Print

Buchwald, Emilie, Pamela R. Fletcher, and Martha Roth, eds. *Transforming a Rape Culture*. Minneapolis: Milkweed Editions, 1993. This collection of essays about the culture of violence in this country, written by men and women, is a good foundational resource for adults.

Maine, Margo. *Body Wars: Making Peace with Women's Bodies.* Carlsbad, CA: Gürze Books, 2000. This book's chapter 11, "Violence Against Women: The Deadliest War," is a good overview of the types of violence that afflict women. It includes quotes by men and women and, like all chapters in the book, strategies for change.

Strauss, Susan, with Pamela Espeland. *Sexual Harassment and Teens: A Program for Positive Change.* Minneapolis: Free Spirit Publishing, 1992. This resource has a complete unit on sexual harassment, with excellent activities, handouts, and in-depth information about sexual harassment in schools and workplaces.

U.S. Bishops' Committees on Marriage and Family Life and on Women in Society and in the Church. *When I Call for Help: A Pastoral Response to Domestic Violence Against Women* (Washington, DC: National Conference of Catholic Bishops [NCCB], United States Catholic Conference, Secretariat for Family, Laity, Women and Youth, 1992). This document can be ordered from the NCCB by calling 202-541-3000, or it can be downloaded from *www.nccbuscc.org/laity/help.htm.*

Internet

Sexual Harassment

www.wgby.org. WGBY public television station, Springfield, Massachusetts. This Web site contains a lesson plan called "Flirting or Hurting? Sexual Harassment in Schools," based on a video by the same name. Information about ordering the video can be found on the Web site.

Domestic Violence and Teen Dating Violence

www.edc.org/WomensEquity. Women's Educational Equity Act Equity Resource Center. This site and its sponsoring organization provide educational materials for schools and parents about sexual harassment and dating violence. The center also offers a technical assistance line on a range of related topics: 800-225-3088.

www.menovercomingviolence.org/youth.html. Men Overcoming Violence. The mailing address and phone number for the organization sponsoring this site are 1385 Mission Street, Suite 300, San Francisco, CA 94103, 415-626-6683.

www.rape101.com. This is an excellent Web site for older teens and adults. It is a good resource for handouts and teaching strategies as well as facts about violence against girls.

Background Information

Violence permeates our culture. No one is immune to its effects, but women and girls suffer in ways that are unique to their gender. The vulnerability of girls and women is not a new phenomenon, but rather rooted throughout human history.

Since early biblical times, girls and women have suffered as the sexual property of men. Lot offered his daughters to his guests to be sexually exploited (Gen. 19:

1–26), Dinah was first raped by a foreigner who fell in love with her, and then avenged violently by her brothers (Gen. 30:19–21; Genesis, chapter 34; Gen. 46:15), and Tamar was raped by her half-brother, David's firstborn son (2 Sam. 13:1–37). Esther came to the attention of the king because of her beauty, but only after Queen Vashti was deposed for refusing her husband's command to parade before his guests at a banquet (Esther, chapters 1–2).

Those ancient stories remind us of the struggles of women throughout history who have been treated as legitimate spoils of war, property to be bartered, and submissive marriage partners to be dominated. Women in the twenty-first century still face violence that threatens their emotional, mental, and physical well-being. Today, we name those violations of human dignity sexual harassment, rape, and domestic violence. Although often related to sexual acts, violence against women and girls is primarily motivated by the desire to control and dominate.

The facts of violence are startling in a culture where long-time patterns of misogyny (hatred of women) are reinforced by the media, which have turned sex and violence into entertainment. "The American Psychological Association warns that 'repeated exposure of scenes of violence against women in movies and TV creates a callousness toward women in both males and females'" (Susan Strauss with Pamela Espeland, *Sexual Harassment and Teens*, p. 19). Consider these facts:

- On average, each year between 1992 and 1996, about one million women and girls over age twelve experienced violence, including rape, sexual assault, robbery, aggravated assault, and simple assault, by a current or former intimate partner.
- Domestic violence is the leading cause of injury to women.
- Half of the female murder victims each year are killed by a male partner.
- Seventy-eight percent of rape victims know their rapist.

(Adapted from Margo Maine, *Body Wars*, pp. 151–152)

The continuum of sexual violence can begin with mild teasing and comments, inappropriate physical touching, or insistent propositions that intimidate or cause discomfort. On the other end of the spectrum are physical and sexual abuse, including rape. Along the continuum are a wide variety of behaviors that are harmful to victims.

Adolescent girls are particularly vulnerable to sexual violence. Thirty-two percent of rapes occur when the victim is between ages eleven and seventeen (Mary Pipher, *Reviving Ophelia*, p. 219). One difficulty for girls is that there is no established or easy way to stop a sexual encounter (p. 208). Drops in self-esteem during adolescence contribute to the problem, as girls often blame themselves, discount their feelings, and fear the societal consequences if they dare to report violence. Though they cannot always name sexual offenses as harassment or violence, girls describe feeling angry, confused, and ashamed immediately following them, and for a long time afterward (Strauss with Espeland, p. 3).

Unfortunately, religion has often been the basis for sexism and domination of women. In their pastoral letter *When I Call for Help: A Pastoral Response to Domestic Violence Against Women*, the U.S. Bishops' Committees on Marriage and Family Life and on Women in Society and in the Church caution about the use of the Scriptures to defend the subjugation of women. Some people actually take biblical texts out of context and distort them to support their right to use violence against women. The bishops clearly state that "violence against women, in the home or outside the home, is *never* justified. Violence in any form—physical, sexual, psychological, or verbal—is sinful."

The pastoral letter points out that throughout the Scriptures, beginning with Genesis, runs the theme that women and men are created in God's image. In his apostolic letter *On the Dignity and Vocation of Women* (*Mulieris Dignitatem,* 1989), Pope John Paul II states that "both man and woman are human beings to an equal degree." The example of Jesus is a model for the mutual respect that women and men should have for each other. Jesus respected the dignity of women, going out of his way to help the most vulnerable women. John Paul II reminds us that "Christ's way of acting, the Gospel of word and deeds, is a consistent protest against whatever offends the dignity of women."

Raising the consciousness of girls and women about the potential dangers of violence in their life can empower them to name and speak against behaviors that put them at risk and keep them from being the persons God created them to be.

Notes

Use this space to jot ideas, reminders, and additional resources.

Building Blocks in Understanding Teen Dating Violence

Violence is common in dating relationships. Studies show that 41 percent of high school students have been involved in dating violence—usually in long-term dating relationships. Patterns of violence in a dating relationship tend to follow the patterns of violence that the young person experienced or witnessed as a child with her or his parents. (Adapted from Julia Ahlers, Barbara Allaire, and Carl Koch, Growing in Christian Morality, p. 204)

These simple building blocks can help you avoid, recognize, or leave an abusive relationship:

1. You are not alone. Our society often glorifies violence, but then looks the other way and rejects those who are victims of violence. Because of that attitude, many people are so ashamed of being battered that they will not tell even their closest friends. The abuser often isolates the victim or threatens the victim with harm if the victim does tell anyone. As a result, many victims think that they are the only one involved with an abuser. It is a great relief to find out there are many others dealing with abuse.

2. The abuse is not your fault. Common phrases of an abuser are, "You made me do it," "You pressed my buttons," and "You've got to learn who's boss." All too often, the abuser will blame the victim for the abuse. The guilt placed on the victim is a tremendous burden and is the number one cause for lower self-image in victims. The perpetrator is always responsible for his or her actions. The abuse is not the fault of the victim.

3. Verbal abuse often precedes physical abuse. Language that belittles, shames, or threatens can damage a person emotionally and psychologically. Verbal abuse is often the first step toward physical abuse. Like physical abuse, constant put-downs and threats are motivated by a need to dominate and control another person by damaging her or his self-worth.

4. If it feels scary, it's abuse. If you are touched in a way that is scary to you, that is abuse. If you are touched in a way that feels uncomfortable to you, that is abuse. If you are touched in a way that feels bad to you, that is abuse.

5. Get some help and support for yourself. Most abusers refuse to seek help because they do not realize how bad their problem is. Victims often feel too embarrassed or scared to seek help. They also may not realize how bad the problem is. If you are abused or are abusing others, get help from organizations like teen health centers, your local battered women's program, crisis lines, a counselor, or a mental health professional.

(Adapted from "Four Building Blocks in Understanding Teen Dating Violence," at *www.rape101.com/handouts/understanding_teen_dating_violence.htm,* 9 November 2000.)

Myths and Realities of Acquaintance Rape

Myth	*Reality*
Only crazed strangers commit rape.	Most women are raped by acquaintances whom people consider normal.
A woman who gets raped deserves it, especially if she agreed to go to the man's house or ride in his car.	No one, male or female, deserves to be raped. Going to a man's house or riding in his car does not mean a woman has agreed to have sex with him.
Women who do not fight back have not been raped.	A woman has been raped when she is forced to have sex against her will, whether or not she resists.
If no gun or knife is used, a woman has not been raped.	It is rape whether the rapist uses a weapon or his fists, verbal threats, drugs, alcohol, physical isolation, or simply the weight of his body.
It is not really rape if the victim was not a virgin.	Rape is rape, even if the woman was not a virgin, even if she had willingly had sex with the man before. Rape can happen between a man and woman married to each other.
If a woman lets a man buy her dinner or pay for a movie, she owes him sex.	No one owes sex as a payment to anyone else, no matter how expensive the date.
Agreeing to kiss or make out with a man means agreeing to have intercourse with him.	Everyone has the right to say no to sexual activity, regardless of what has preceded it, and to have their no respected.
When men are sexually aroused, they need to have sex; they cannot help themselves once they are turned on.	Men do not physically need to have sex after becoming aroused, any more than women do. Moreover, men are still able to control themselves even after becoming physically excited.
Women lie about being raped, especially when they accuse men they date or other acquaintances.	Rape really happens—to people you know, by people you know. To falsely accuse another person of rape is a serious matter and can never be justified.
If a woman gets drunk or is using drugs, it is her own fault if she gets raped.	A woman's own diminished physical or mental state is no excuse for someone to rape her. Sex without full consent is rape. It is important to know that many rapes do occur while at least one of the people involved is under the influence of alcohol or drugs. Protect yourself by avoiding substance abuse or friends who need alcohol or drugs to have a good time.

(Adapted from Ms. Foundation for Education and Communication, *I Never Called It Rape: The Ms. Report on Recognizing, Fighting, and Surviving Date and Acquaintance Rape,* as excerpted at "Myths About Acquaintance Rape," *www.rape101.com/myths.htm,* 8 November 2000. Copyright © 1988 by the Ms. Foundation for Education and Communication, and Sarah Lazin Books.

Why Victims Don't Report Sexual Harassment

Read the reasons below, and record each one under the correct heading on your group's newsprint. Also add to the newsprint any other valid reasons that you think of.

- They blame themselves.
- They feel helpless, hopeless, and/or powerless.
- They don't know how to report the harassment.
- They think that their complaint won't be taken seriously.
- They don't trust their own perceptions of what happened—maybe they "misunderstood."
- They don't want to "rock the boat."
- They are afraid of the harasser or others (example: the harasser's friends or family).
- They don't trust "the system."
- They don't think their school/workplace will support them if they report the harassment.
- They don't think their friends will support them.
- They feel embarrassed.
- They don't think that reporting will make any difference; they don't believe that anything will be done about the harassment or the harasser.
- They don't want to get the harasser into trouble.
- They are prevented or blocked by sex role stereotyping.
- They are prevented or blocked by victim behavior.

(Susan Strauss with Pamela Espeland, *Sexual Harassment and Teens: A Program for Positive Change* [Minneapolis: Free Spirit Publishing, 1992], page 117. Copyright © 1992 by Susan Strauss.

What to Do if It Happens to You

Follow the sexual harassment policy and procedure that are used by your school, district, or workplace. If there are no existing policy and procedure, use this process:

Step 1. Communicate to your harasser verbally or in writing. Clearly state the behavior, what you feel about it, and the expectation that it be stopped. If you choose, get help and support from a friend or a parent, professional, or other trusted adult.

Step 2. If the behavior is repeated, go to a person in authority, such as a principal, counselor, complaint manager, or supervisor. Document exactly what happened. Give a copy of your written record to the authority and keep one for yourself. Your documentation should include the following information:
- what happened
- when it happened
- where it happened
- who did the harassing
- who the witnesses were
- what you said or did in response
- how your harasser responded to you
- how you felt about the harassment

Step 3. If the behavior is repeated again, go to a person in higher authority, such as a school board member, the superintendent of schools, or the company president. Keep documenting the behavior.

(Adapted from Susan Strauss with Pamela Espeland, *Sexual Harassment and Teens: A Program for Positive Change* [Minneapolis: Free Spirit Publishing, 1992], page 118. Copyright © 1992 by Susan Strauss.

The Truth About Beauty

Challenging the Culture of the Perfect Body

Springboard Activity

The Me I Am

This activity examines body image and eating disorders among adolescent girls. The girls explore and reflect on the cultural factors that lead to poor self-esteem and unhealthy attitudes about physical appearance. They are reminded that by calling us to self-respect and self-love, our faith reinforces the idea that we are made in the image of God. This activity is useful with both younger and older teens.

Preparation
○ Copy resource 6, "Real Words from Real Girls," cut it apart as scored, and clip the quotes together in a set. You will need one set of quotes for every six to eight girls.
○ Cut blank strips of paper, one for each participant.

1. Distribute the blank slips of paper. Ask the girls to copy and complete the following sentence-starters on opposite sides of the paper. Explain that their answers will be shared with the group but will remain anonymous, and caution them not to put their name or any other identifying information on their paper.
⊚ What I like most about being the age I am is . . .
⊚ What I fear most is . . .
Collect the completed papers and hang on to them for step 3 of this activity.

2. Create small groups of six to eight girls. Place a set of quotes from resource 6 facedown in the center of each group and announce the following instructions in your own words:

@ Each participant in turn picks a quote and reads it aloud. The other group members respond by showing from zero to five fingers. Zero fingers, that is, a fist, means, "I cannot relate to that at all." Five fingers means, "That's exactly the way I've felt!" The person who reads the quote records the group members' responses on the back of the quote. The process continues around the circle until all the quotes have been read.

Ask for a volunteer in each group to begin.

3. While the girls are working in small groups, read their sentence-starter papers, quickly arranging them into common categories such as dating, academics, driving, family, freedom, school, body, and violence.

Make two columns on newsprint or the board, using the sentence-starters as headings. Under each heading, write the general categories of the girls' responses and the number of responses that correspond to each category.

4. Gather the girls and ask for feedback from their small groups. Discuss which quotes describe their own experiences and which are far removed from their life. Then display your tally of their responses to the sentence-starters. Share your own observations and ask the girls if anything about the responses surprises them.

5. Share with the group some of the background information near the end of this theme, which focuses on eating disorders and body image. Invite discussion, feedback, and insights.

6. Close by inviting the girls to write a short note to their body from God. They might begin, "I'm the God who created your body, and I'd like to tell you that . . ."

Consider collecting the notes and reading them anonymously at subsequent sessions or compiling them into a resource or handout. If you do that, take care not to include anything that might identify an author.

Additional Activities

Impossible Bodies

This activity works with both younger and older teens. However, younger teens might need action ideas to get them started. No matter what age girls you work with, be sure that they focus on the task and not on the media.

Preparation
○ Set up three stations by arranging the girls' tables and chairs, or desks, in three approximately equal groups or circles. Place the following items at the stations:
  • *Station 1.* teen magazines, a scissors, a stapler, index cards, pens, a sheet of newsprint, a marker, and a sheet of paper that says the following:

Directions. Locate advertisements that use models who have "impossible bodies." Cut out the ads; staple each one to an index card; and write on the card the name of the magazine, the page number of the ad, and the name of the company sponsoring the ad.

- *Station 2.* two pieces of newsprint, a marker, entertainment magazines and newspaper ads for movies, and a sheet of paper that says the following:

    Directions. On one sheet of newsprint, list movie celebrities (male and female) that you think have "impossible bodies." Use the materials provided for ideas, or think of your own examples.

- *Station 3.* two sheets of newsprint, a marker, television guides or magazines, and a sheet of paper that says the following:

    Directions. On one sheet of newsprint, list television celebrities (male and female) that you think have "impossible bodies," and the shows they appear in. Use the materials provided for ideas, or come up with your own examples.

○ You may want to use upbeat music to monitor the time and facilitate movement from one station to the next. If so, set up a CD or tape player with appropriate recordings.

1. Invite the girls to sit at any table or desk, without moving any chairs. When everyone is in place, tell them they have 7 minutes to complete the directions at their station.

2. After 7 minutes, direct the girls to move individually to one of the other two stations, mixing up the groups as they do so. Instruct them to leave the results of their work—the ads or newsprint lists—at the station they are departing.

When everyone is settled again, tell the girls that they now have 5 minutes to brainstorm actions to address the problem of "impossible bodies" in the medium represented at their station. Note that one girl in each group should write the ideas on the clean sheet of newsprint.

3. After 5 minutes, direct the girls to move individually to the station they have not yet been to. Tell them to review the list of actions at their station and to each vote for the two that they think are the most doable. Ask someone at each station to tally the votes and to scratch out the ideas with the least number of votes, keeping only the top three.

4. Call someone from each station to report the station's top three ideas. Decide as a group on one or two ideas that you will do together or individually. Follow up by actually planning and carrying out the action or actions.

Beauty Shop

In a school setting, consider using a particular day of the week for one or two girls to receive the "beauty shop" treatment. In other settings, you might arrange for one or two girls to be treated at the beginning or end of each meeting.

This activity works best for a group of girls who meet regularly and know one another fairly well, whether they are in middle school or high school. For groups of girls who are not very familiar with one another, consider the first two options and actions listed later in this theme.

Preparation

○ Assign someone to be the receptionist, making appointments for one or two girls each day or meeting.
○ Arrange the girls' desks or chairs in a circle, inserting one special chair for the beauty shop client. Consider adding props such as nail polish, curlers, a hair dryer, and mirrors.

1. Invite the girl who has the current beauty shop appointment to sit in the special seat. Provide paper, and pens or pencils, for everyone and ask them to write a three- or four-sentence affirmation about the inner beauty of the girl in the chair. For example, someone might write: "Laura, I think you are beautiful because you always seem to be there when people need you. Your work with community service challenges me. I never pass you in the hall without getting a smile from you." At the same time, the client should think of someone close to her (perhaps a parent, friend, grandparent, godmother, or sibling), and write a note to herself from that person, describing three or four things that person might like about her.

2. Invite each girl to read her finished affirmation to the client. Direct the client to respond to each affirmation with a statement like, "Thank you for recognizing the beauty in me." Also invite the client to read the affirmation she wrote, if she wishes to.

3. Conclude with your own affirmation of the girl and a blessing that may be as simple as, "God, we ask you to bless Laura today, help her recognize her own beauty as we have seen it here, and give her the courage to share her beauty for the sake of a world that so desperately needs to see it."

Steel Magnolias

This activity uses the movie *Steel Magnolias* to encourage the girls to choose mentors who will be positive influences. It also challenges the girls to become mentors for younger girls in their community. Since the movie applications deal with mature themes, this activity works best with high school girls. It is an ideal follow-up to the "Beauty Shop" activity.

Preparation

○ Bring in the movie *Steel Magnolias* (Tri-Star Pictures, distributed by RCA/Columbia Pictures Home Video, 1989, 118 minutes, rated PG).

1. Write the word "mentor" on newsprint or the board. Ask the girls to call out all the words they think of when they see or hear that term, and list their ideas.

2. Share the following information in your own words:
- In the classic epic *Odyssey*, by Homer, Odysseus leaves his son Telemachus with his trusted friend Mentor when he goes off to fight in the Trojan War.
- Athena, the goddess of wisdom, sometimes would take the shape of Mentor and help counsel Telemachus.

3. Show the movie *Steel Magnolias*. A summary of the movie follows for your reference. After the movie, conduct a discussion focusing around questions like the ones below the summary.

Summary: *Steel Magnolias*

Truvy's Beauty Parlor is the setting for a close-knit group of friends who come to share their lives, struggles, and joy in a small Louisiana town. They mentor one another and younger women, such as Annelle and Shelby.

- How does Truvy attempt to mentor Annelle?
- Is Truvy a good mentor? Why or why not?
- How does M'Lynn try to be a mentor and role model for her daughter, Shelby?
- What role do Clairee and Ouiser play in mentoring the others?
- Which character in the movie might be a good personal mentor for you? Why?

A Letter to a Body Part

This activity works best with older girls. It can also be done as a journal activity.

1. Distribute handout 11, "Poem in Which My Legs Are Accepted." Read the poem aloud.

2. Instruct the girls to choose the part of their body that they dislike or complain about the most and write a letter of apology to it. Offer the following directions in your own words:
- Begin your letter with a greeting like, "My dear Hips" or "Dearest Nose." Explain to that body part why you feel so badly about it, and thank it for all the good it has done. This process can help you make peace with that part of your body.

3. If the girls are comfortable doing so, invite them to share their completed letters with the group.

Options and Actions

- Before you conduct the "Beauty Shop" activity, secretly ask one significant person from each girl's life to write a letter affirming her inner beauty. Be sure to let the writer know that you will be reading the letter in front of the whole group. As part of the affirmation process, read the letter.

- For the "Beauty Shop" activity, schedule an appointment to affirm the entire group, with participants finishing the statement, "I think that this group of girls is beautiful because . . ."
- Invite the girls to write thank-you letters to the women who have taught them how to be beautiful—both in appearance and more important, in soul.
- After watching *Steel Magnolias,* divide the girls into groups of three or four, provide paper and art supplies, and challenge the groups each to create a wanted poster advertising for a mentor. Invite each group to share its completed work with everyone.
- Arrange for the girls to lead a group of younger girls in a school, church group, or Scout troop in a session about the joys and struggles of adolescence. Help the young women prepare for the session, advising them to include time for listening to the younger girls' hopes and dreams for the future, and to talk about body image, dieting, and anything else that is age appropriate for the younger group.
- Brainstorm with the girls a list of contemporary Christian women who are known for their good works, such as Thea Bowman, Dorothy Day, Saint Katharine Drexel, Ita Ford, Edith Stein, and Mother Teresa. Assign the girls to research those women, prepare brief written reports on them, and bring in clothes like they wore. On the date the reports are due, hold a Christian fashion show, with the girls taking turns playing the supermodel and the announcer, and the announcer reading the written report as the corresponding model walks the runway. End the show by offering affirmations of the women researched; for example, "Dorothy Day, I think you are beautiful because . . ."
- Find information on the Barbie doll and its impact on the body image of women and girls.
- Instruct the girls to write letters to companies with advertisements that feature "impossible bodies" or media producers who promote unhealthy attitudes about physical appearance through their work.
- Everyone has clothes that make them feel unattractive or uncomfortable, or attractive and at ease. Some clothes even hold good or bad memories. Have the girls bring in an item of clothing or outfit and share the emotions or memories it holds for them.
- Invite young adult women to write the group letters about their own adolescence. A good phrase to help them get started is, "Something I know now that I wish I had known when I was in high school is . . ."

Reflection and Discussion

Journal Questions

- ◉ Imagine you are the mother of a teenage daughter. List all the things you want her to know so that she can have a good and beautiful life.

◎ Think about the parts of your inner self that you would like to change. Write a prayer using this starter: "God, help me make over . . ." Hang this prayer on your mirror as a reminder that true beauty is the radiance of inner truth.

◎ Tom Hanks, in the film *Forrest Gump,* repeats the phrase, "Stupid is as stupid does," meaning that being stupid is the same as acting stupid. It is the same with beauty: To be beautiful is to act in such a way that you make the world beautiful before others. "Doing beauty" takes practice. Select a virtue that you want to focus on, such as patience, honesty, or gratitude. Write about why that virtue is important to you. Say the virtue several times daily. At the end of a week, write about how life has been different since you have focused on that virtue.

Scriptural Connections

• Wis. 7:22–23,25–26 (Real beauty is a reflection of God's goodness.)
• Wis. 8:2–3 (Wisdom is beauty.)
• Sir. 11:1–6 (Appearances may be deceiving.)

WomanWisdom Quotes

Don't go changin'
to try and please me . . .
I love you just the way you are.
                              (Billy Joel)

Sometimes a good feeling from inside is worth much more than a beautician. (Mother Teresa)

The externals are simply so many props; everything we need is within us. (Etty Hillesum)

Prayer

May you awaken to yourself as beautiful
May you know that you are God's beloved delight
May your relationships flourish your growth
And may unconditional love be the soil within which new beginnings are planted
. . . .
May you always recognize "moments" of God's presence
May you continue on the journey of knowing yourself
May you awaken to yourself as loving
May you love your God enough to love yourself
And may you be a face of Christ in this world.
Amen.

(Danielle Rossi, "A Blessing for Girls")

Resource Materials

Print

Cooke, Kaz. *Real Gorgeous: The Truth About Body and Beauty.* New York: W. W. Norton and Co., 1996. This empowering book tells girls and women how to be friends with their bodies. It is packed with jokes, cartoons, and practical ways to find real self-esteem. *Real Gorgeous* is easy to read, relevant, and an indispensable boost for girls and women, ages 1 to 111.

Maine, Margo. *Body Wars: Making Peace with Women's Bodies.* Carlsbad, CA: Gürze Books, 2000. This book covers issues from dieting and weight prejudice to concepts of beauty and ageism to sports, fashion advertising, and propaganda. It also provides practical strategies for activists, educators, and parents, and contains extensive references and appendices.

Internet

www.aabainc.org. American Anorexia Bulimia Association. This site provides general information on eating disorders, including symptoms and medical consequences.

www.about-face.org. About-Face. This site and its sponsoring organization focus on how mass media affect the physical, mental, and emotional well-being of women and girls. The site includes a number of articles by Liz Dittrich, PhD, about eating disorders, body image, and the media. It also provides an extensive bibliography on related topics.

www.dadsanddaughters.org. Dads and Daughters. This site is sponsored by an organization that was begun by fathers of young adolescent girls, who are devoted to the healthy growth of girls and critical analysis of the media. The organization can also be reached at 888-824-3237.

Background Information

by Janet Claussen and Danielle Rossi

Some basic information:

- "What do young girls fear more than cancer, nuclear war, and losing their parents? Getting fat!" (Atlanta Anti-Eating Disorders League [AAEDL] brochure).
- "70% of 5th through 12th grade girls say magazine pictures influence their idea of the perfect body shape" (AAEDL brochure).
- Ninety percent of all girls ages three to eleven have a Barbie doll, an early role model with a figure that is unattainable in real life.
- "By high school, up to 60% of girls are on a diet" (AAEDL brochure).
- "A dieting teen is 8 times more likely to develop an eating disorder than her non-dieting peer" (AAEDL brochure).
- "Today the average fashion model weighs 23% less than the average woman" (AAEDL brochure).

- "In 1992, the ten most popular magazines most commonly read by men and women were reviewed for ads and articles related to weight loss. The women's magazines contained 10.5 times more articles related to dieting and weight loss than the men's magazines" (Andersen and DiDomenico, in Liz Dittrich, comp., "About-Face Facts on the Media").
- "In a society where thinness is equated with success and happiness, nearly every American woman, man and child has suffered at one time or another from issues of weight, body shape and self-image" (American Anorexia Bulimia Association, "General Information on Eating Disorders").
- "Beauty is the defining characteristic for American women. . . . The pressure to be beautiful is most intense in early adolescence. Girls worry about their clothes, makeup, skin and hair. But most of all they worry about their weight" (Mary Pipher, *Reviving Ophelia,* p. 183).
- "It's difficult to be a healthy eater in this country. Unhealthy food is everywhere, and we are encouraged to consume without thinking of the consequences" (Pipher, p. 180).
- The irony of a society in which immediate gratification has led to high levels of obesity is that some people are actually "dying to be thin." More than five million Americans suffer from eating disorders, and one thousand women die from complications of those disorders each year (National Institute of Mental Health).
- "The popular idea that eating disorders are mainly a problem among the wealthy has now been disproved by several studies. In recent years it has been found that eating disorders are now also occurring among women in lower [socioeconomic] groups" (Liz Dittrich, comp., "About-Face Facts on SES, Ethnicity, and the Thin Ideal").

Anorexia nervosa is a preoccupation with thinness that leads to excessive weight loss. Bulimia nervosa, the most common eating disorder, involves eating and then purging the contents of the stomach. A third eating disorder involves binge eating, leading to obesity. Libraries and the Internet have hundreds of resources devoted to the eating problems that afflict girls, starting in their adolescence. For danger signs and medical consequences, the Web site for the American Anorexia Bulimia Association, *www.aabainc.org,* is particularly helpful.

Ninety to 95 percent of those with eating disorders are female, and adolescent girls tend to be particularly susceptible. Teachers, counselors, and youth leaders are called to minister to girls in ways that may help prevent or mitigate low self-esteem, depression, and eating problems associated with body image dissatisfaction.

While the media and pop culture portray happiness with the empty promises of a perfect appearance and unlimited material possessions, our faith reminds us that true happiness can only come from within. No matter how much we work out, diet, and try new hairstyles, we will not change how we feel about ourselves unless we tend to the inner spaces of our being. Caring for the exterior is a wonderful thing, as long as it is done because we love our body and want the best for it. Poor body image has less to do with how we look on the outside and more to do with how we feel about ourselves in places that only God sees.

True beauty is the humility that comes with knowing ourselves, our truth, and with that understanding, knowing God in a deep and almost unexplainable way. Uncovering the secrets that lie within our heart is hard work but extremely worthwhile. We must tend to our inner selves with the same vigor with which we tend to our exterior selves.

Just as running a marathon requires proper training, achieving a sense of inner well-being requires prayer, virtues, and holistic living. The sense of personal freedom that develops when a female begins to truly know herself is attractive to those who meet her. A female at peace with herself radiates and invites others into her company. This is true beauty, the radiance of truth.

Notes

Use this space to jot ideas, reminders, and additional resources.

Real Words from Real Girls

Because I am a young woman I feel I always have to look good. When I page through *Seventeen* magazine or *YM* I get a sense that because I don't look like any of the models, there is no way I am going to have any relationships with guys. I know this is wrong for me to think like this, but I am always reminded every day who I should try to look like and what I should buy to look good. In school I have to cope with wearing the right clothes, looking cute, getting good grades and always being nice to everyone. I sometimes feel like I can't speak my mind. (Laurie)

When I started here (from an all-girls' school) I walked tall, talked to anybody (you couldn't shut me up), and had good grades, mainly because of my class participation. Now I'm distracted, quiet, and I've stopped talking in class so much. I've watched myself sink into a hole where boys are on the top and girls are on the bottom. Girls are being ignored because of their gender and that is sexual discrimination of some sort. . . . girls doubt themselves. (Beth)

I know sometimes girls will hold back on their ideas (or answers) because they are afraid the boys will laugh at them and then they will feel stupid. There is a lot of competition between boys and girls about who is smarter. Guys make fun of the way girls look, so girls become paranoid about their hair, makeup . . . it will never be enough. (Marta)

Society puts such great emphasis on what you look like that it drives my self-esteem down. I feel I am always expected to look like everyone in magazine ads. The models don't even look that good—anyone could with an airbrush. (Christina)

Not a day goes by that, while I'm in school, I don't run to the mirror and check my hair or my face. Then, when I get to the mirror, of course I don't like what I see. I think to myself, "Maybe I could be thinner," or, "I wish I were prettier," when I really should just be comfortable with who I am because I am special and unique. (Gina)

I wish there weren't any competition about clothes, boys or looks. There is a lot of competition in this school and I don't like it. I never feel that I can wear what I want because I feel like people are going to look at me weird or talk about my clothes and judge me as a person. I feel you have to have the clothes everybody's wearing or have the right stuff or you're not good enough. (Beth)

I think the most difficult thing I have to deal with in school is the expectation for girls to be perfect. It is such an impossible task because everyone has their own interpretation of the "perfect girl" and it seems that you are always being labeled as something different because you don't always meet these expectations. I believe this is really hard on teenage girls in general, because then, most of the time we spend our teenage years trying to please everyone else and we forget about our own needs. Therefore, we are never really satisfied with ourselves because we are too busy constantly trying to meet these complicated, impossible goals. (Noelle)

I was just overwhelmed with what I thought other people wanted me to be: smart, outgoing, hot, thin, "the ideal female." It started with makeup, doing my hair, dressing a certain way, doing things certain ways, being smart but not too smart. . . . Then it went on to dieting—my major downfall. I thought if I lost weight I would get anyone I wanted. I would be perfect, finally. I let my weight, my appearance, food and exercise become an obsession. It may have only lasted a year, but that is all I can remember from that period. I got suckered into thinking that Kathleen doesn't matter any more, what Kathleen thinks doesn't count, all that matters is what guys think. (Kathleen)

Poem in Which My Legs Are Accepted

by Kathleen Fraser

Legs!
How we have suffered each other,
never meeting the standards of magazines
                              or official measurements.

I have hung you from trapezes,
        sat you on wooden rollers,
        pulled and pushed you
                              with the anxiety of taffy,
and still, you are yourselves!

Most obvious imperfection, blight on my fantasy life,
strong,
plump,
never to be skinny
or even hinting of the svelte beauties in history books
                              or Sears catalogues.

. . . .

Legs!
O that was the year we did acrobatics in the annual gym show.
How you split for me!
                One-handed cartwheels
                from this end of the gymnasium to the other,
                ending in double splits,
legs you flashed in blue rayon slacks my mother bought for the
        occasion
and tho you were confidently swinging along,
the rest of me blushed at the sound of clapping.

Legs!
How I have worried about you, not able to hide you.
embarrassed at beaches, in highschool
                        when the cheerleaders' slim brown legs
                                spread all over
                                the sand
                                with the perfection
                                of bamboo.
I hated you, and still you have never given out on me.

With you
I have risen to the top of blue waves,
with you
I have carried food home as a loving gift
                                when my arms began
                                unjelling like madrilene.

(In Sandra Eagleton, PhD, *Women in Literature: Life Stages Through Stories,
Poems, and Plays* [Englewood Cliffs, NJ: Prentice-Hall, 1988], pages 109–110.
Copyright © 1988 by Prentice-Hall.)

The Color Purple

Challenging the Culture of Voiceless Women

Springboard Activity

Lost and Found Voices

This activity uses two clips from the movie *The Color Purple* to explore self-esteem and loss of voice among women. It is an ideal companion to the first springboard activity in this manual, "Losing Your Voice, Getting Your Man," on pages 19 to 20. Based on Alice Walker's novel by the same name, the film focuses on the experience of African American women, although its issues of oppression and domestic violence can be found in every culture throughout the ages.

Be aware that this movie has been criticized for depicting the male characters as primarily abusive. Also, the movie is rated PG-13, mostly because of violence and strong language. We recommend it for older adolescent girls, with adults helping them to get beneath the surface and recognize the theme of voice, its loss and its recovery.

Preparation

◎ For clip 1, queue the movie *The Color Purple* (Warner Brothers, 1985, 154 minutes, rated PG-13) to about 81 minutes, where Celie is packing to leave with Shug. For clip 2, queue it to about 121 minutes, the dinner scene.

◎ Review the entire movie so that you are able to put the clips in context. Review the two clips in light of this activity plan.

◎ Make enough copies of resource 7, "The Color Purple," so that you can give each girl one question, and cut the copies apart as scored.

1. Ask for a show of hands from those who have seen the movie *The Color Purple*. Invite one person to give a short summary of the plot, or offer your own summary, providing a context for the two clips that you will show.

2. Tell the girls that they will watch two scenes from the movie. Begin the first clip, and stop it after about 2 minutes, when Celie collapses in the road as Shug drives off. Then lead a discussion around questions like these:

- ◉ What did you notice in this clip?
- ◉ What kind of person does Celie appear to be?
- ◉ Why is Celie so afraid?
- ◉ What, do you think, does Celie want to say to Shug? What does she actually say?
- ◉ What do you think of Shug's question to Celie, "Cat got your tongue?"
- ◉ What is Albert's reaction to Celie's wanting to leave?
- ◉ How does he react when she collapses?

3. Show the second clip, where the family has gathered for dinner, which runs about 10 minutes. Solicit the girls' general reactions to the scene. Then randomly distribute question slips from resource 7. Be sure that all the girls have at least one question to focus on and that all the questions are distributed. Replay the clip, asking the girls to pay special attention to the part that addresses their question or questions. Use the questions as a starting point for analyzing the scene and for further discussion, beginning with question 1 and proceeding consecutively.

4. Conclude this activity by emphasizing these points in your own words:

- ◉ Women of all races and ages have suffered in situations of silence and secondary status. Minority women often face additional obstacles to equality because of their race and economic status. All people—men and women—need to empower one another to become the kind of persons God created them to be. As we become more conscious of things in our culture that contribute to the exploitation of others, we are called to use our voice to change the world around us.

Options and Actions

- With the girls, watch the scene toward the end of the movie where Shug sings "Maybe God Is Tryin' to Tell You Somethin'." This scene of reconciliation between father and daughter is a powerful example of conversion. Note that the daughter approaches the father. Compare this scene with the story of the prodigal son in Luke 15:11–24. Use the two stories as a springboard for discussion of how God communicates with us through the voices and actions of others.
- Invite the girls to bring in items that are purple. Use red and blue pastels, paints, crayons, or pencils to demonstrate the colors that blend to make purple. Then provide an assortment of colors, including plenty of red and blue, and encourage the girls to see how many colors of purple they can create. List the places that purple is found in nature. Think about songs that refer to purple. Research quotes that have to do with purple. Hold a celebration of the color purple.

- Use a concordance to find references to purple in the Bible, and a Bible encyclopedia to find out about the symbolism of purple in biblical times. Point out the liturgical symbolism of purple in the church seasons. Explore these questions with your group: What is the symbolism of purple in secular culture? Does purple hold special significance for the African American culture? Ask the girls to share their favorite color and its significance.

- Read Alice Walker's novel *The Color Purple* with the girls. Be aware that it contains profane language, sexuality, and incest. However, individual chapters provide rich material for discussion. About three-fourths of the way into the book, Celie's letter to her sister Nettie is a powerful exploration of the existence of God and images of God.

- Use the scriptural connections for this theme to find out more about the culture of women in the Bible. The Scripture stories provide a glimpse of the various roles that women played during biblical times. Rachel and Leah face circumstances similar to those of Nettie and Celie in the beginning of the movie; Dinah's status as property is not unlike Celie's; and Lydia could be a role model for Celie in her later years. Have the girls role-play Rebekah, Leah, and Lydia conversing with Celie and Nettie. (If you have a large group, you might include Rachel and Dinah in this role-play.)

- The oppression of women depicted in the movie was not unusual for the time period of the story, regardless of race or socioeconomic class. Many women today continue to suffer from similar conditions of secondary status in the family and society. Find out more about females around the world by researching the Beijing World Conference on Women and its statements about women and the status of girls.

- Find out how domestic violence affects women and girls in this country. Bring in a speaker from a shelter for battered women or a legal advocate for battered women, to talk about the problem and how it affects all women—and men.

- One subplot in the film involves Sofia, who is jailed for years. Research the status of women in prison in this country, addressing questions like these: What are common reasons why women are sent to prison? What happens to their children? Guide a service project that involves writing to women in prison, or visiting them or their children.

Reflection and Discussion

Journal Questions

- Reflect on the old ad slogan, "You've come a long way, baby." Write or draw about how different your life might have been fifty or a hundred years ago.

- How does a culture of violence affect you? What opportunities do you have to promote nonviolence in your community?

- What advice would you give to girls who find themselves in relationships that seem to be controlling or abusive?

֍ Celie struggles with the concept of a God who would abandon her to such abuse. Imagine God's response to her by writing her a letter from God.

Scriptural Connections

- Gen. 25:19–28; 27:1–29 (Rebekah)
- Genesis, chapters 28–35 (Rachel and Leah)
- Genesis, chapter 34 (Dinah)
- Acts 16:11–15,40 (Lydia)

WomanWisdom Quotes

Silence and invisibility go hand in hand with powerlessness. (Audre Lorde)

When there is violence against any person in society, because he or she is different, it threatens us all. Only by speaking out are any of us safe. (Madeleine Kunin)

It is part of the amazing originality of Christ that there is to be found in his teaching no word whatever which suggests a difference in the spiritual ideals, the spheres, or the potentialities of men and women. (Maude Royden)

The men who are brought up to respect women, the men who are brought up to respect the earth as woman, think of the earth and the woman as one and the same, are the real men. (Cecilia Mitchell)

Prayer

Use the service based on the movie *The Color Purple* in the Voices manual *Prayer: Celebrating and Reflecting with Girls* (available in 2002). Or use this procedure for a prayer service:

Prepare a prayer space using a candle, the book *The Color Purple,* the cover from the videotape *The Color Purple,* a purple cloth, and fabric with an African motif. Invite the girls into the prayer space and call them to silence. Light the candle. Slowly and prayerfully read excerpts from Celie's second letter to Nettie in the book *The Color Purple.* The letter begins with an explanation of why Celie no longer writes to God, and is located about two-thirds of the way through the book.

Notes

Use this space to jot ideas, reminders, and additional resources.

The Color Purple

Question 1. Why, do you think, does Celie find her voice? How do you feel about what she says to Albert when she first speaks up at the dinner table?

Question 2. How did you feel when Celie holds the knife at Albert's throat? What, do you think, would have happened to Celie if she had used violence against Albert? Is violence against oppressors ever justified?

Question 3. For years, Albert has been keeping letters from Celie's sister Nettie hidden from her. Why, do you think, has Albert wanted to block the relationship between Nettie and her sister? Do you think that sisters often have a special bond of friendship?

Question 4. Sofia has just been released from years in jail. She got in trouble for speaking up for herself to the mayor's wife, who was white, and then knocking down the mayor himself. Why does Celie blame Harpo for Sofia's trouble?

Question 5. What part does money play in Celie's situation and decision to leave? What role does economics play in abused women's lives?

Question 6. What is Sofia trying to tell Celie? How has Sofia's strong voice caused her trouble and pain? How does prison or jail affect the spirit of those who are imprisoned?

Question 7. How was Celie a reflection of God for Sofia? How influential do you think friendships with other girls or women are? What are some typical ways that girls help others to feel better or more confident? In what ways are girl-girl relationships sometimes harmful or hurtful?

Question 8. What is so important about Mary Agnes's statement about her name? Why is a person's name important? How is Mary Agnes empowered by the other women in this scene? How do mothers and older women influence girls' development of self-esteem?

Question 9. What does Albert's father's message to Albert imply about the role of men in the family? How do gender roles in society often keep men from being the kind of people God created them to be?

Question 10. We see several fathers throughout the movie: Celie's father, Albert, Albert's father, and Shug's father. Where are the mothers of Celie, Shug, Sofia, and Albert? How does the absence of mothers affect the family in the movie?

Question 11. How does Albert acknowledge the power of a woman's voice when he compares Celie to Shug? How does hearing verbal abuse make you feel as a bystander? How do you think it affects the children who are at the table in the movie? Is verbal abuse as harmful as physical abuse?

Question 12. Albert lists what he perceives as Celie's shortcomings. What are they? How do race, gender, appearance, and economics affect a person's situation in life? Is Celie's situation still common in our society? the world? What are some other factors that keep people marginalized or oppressed?

Question 13. How did you feel when Celie was leaving with Shug? Compare that departure with the one in the first clip. What are some ways that girls and women lose their voices today, or fail to use them?

Part B

Promoting Positive Cultures

Pinpointing Your Passion

Promoting a Culture of Vocation

Girls need to be encouraged to examine their dreams and zero in on what will be most life-giving to them. That means going beyond choosing a future career, and really getting at the question of what brings joy to their life. This theme uses discussion and a movie to encourage the girls to determine where their passion lies and why they should develop it.

Because this theme is conceptually advanced, it is probably most effective with girls in high school. However, middle school girls will benefit from it if it is guided in a way that is age appropriate.

Springboard Activity

Living Authentically

Preparation
○ Make a sign displaying the following question: "Is the life you are living the life that wants to live inside you?" (adapted from Parker J. Palmer, *Let Your Life Speak,* front flap).
○ Review and bring in the movie *Little Women* (Columbia Pictures, 1994, 119 minutes, rated PG), and think about how it fits with this theme.

1. Post the sign you made, and ask the girls to think about how they would answer the question on it. Allow a couple of minutes for reflection, then ask for volunteers to share their thoughts. Next make the following points in your own words:
   ◈ The question is truly about vocation. Vocation is living faithfully as the person you are called to be by your Creator and your Baptism.
   ◈ The word *vocation* comes from the Latin word for "voice," *voca.* We must listen carefully for the voice within us—the voice of God—to help shape who we are and who we are called to be.

2. Create groups of three or four people and give each group a sheet of newsprint and markers. Encourage the girls to brainstorm movies, television shows, and books in which a female character does not live authentically, that is, lives the way someone else wants her to and does not follow her true vocation. Ask them to underline the situations where this happens just because the character is female. When they are done, call someone from each group to share their list with everyone and to explain why their group put certain items on it. Draw attention to any connections and similarities between the work of different groups.

3. Describe the following dilemmas in your own words, or name the characters and ask the girls to offer their ideas about each one and her vocation:

- In the Walt Disney movie *Pocahontas* (1995), the heroine wonders whether she should marry as her father wishes or pursue her own dreams. She chooses to wait and see what lies "just around the river bend," and finds the life that she must live.
- In the Walt Disney movie *Mulan* (1998), the heroine disguises herself as a boy so that she can fight in place of her father. This is a matter of honor to her.
- In the movie *Yentl* (MGM/UA Studios, 1983), Barbra Streisand's character disguises herself as a man in order to study the Torah.
- The classic novel from Louisa May Alcott, *Little Women,* speaks to the theme of finding the life meant for you. For example, Jo March longs to be a writer and publishes her work under a male pseudonym.

4. Show the movie *Little Women* to the girls. Ask them to write down any lines that speak to the theme of vocation and living authentically.

5. Using questions like the ones that follow, lead a discussion about the movie:

- What lines did you write down as you watched the movie? Why did you choose them?
- What societal norms and expectations are evident in the movie?
- How did the mother, Marmee, challenge those standards?
- How did Marmee encourage her daughters to grow in self-esteem and aspire to their dreams?
- What dreams did Jo, Meg, Amy, and Beth have?
- What risks did Jo take in order to live authentically?
- What male relationships supported and encouraged the March women's dreams?

6. Close the activity by encouraging the girls to live authentically and to focus on the voice within them that calls them to fullness of life. Emphasize that that voice is surely the voice of God, who created them to live the life that wants to live in them.

Options and Actions

- Form small groups, and direct each one to develop and present a role-play that offers advice to fifth- or sixth-grade girls from one of the media characters identified by the girls in step 2 of the springboard activity. Explain that the role-play can be an interview, a scene from a play, a talk show segment, or any other format.
- Show clips from the other movies mentioned in the springboard activity, or encourage the girls to view those movies, and instruct the girls to write a reflection on how each movie portrays the theme of vocation and authentic living.
- If the girls have participated in the activity "Losing Your Voice, Getting Your Man," on pages 19 to 20, ask them to apply the theme of vocation and authentic living to the situation of Ariel as illustrated in the song "Part of Your World" in the Walt Disney movie *The Little Mermaid*.
- Give each girl a blank piece of paper and tell everyone to draw three large circles that overlap in the center of the paper. Tell them to write their greatest gift or strength in the first circle, what they most enjoy doing in the second, and something the world really needs in the third. Invite the girls to share their completed circles and talk about choices they might make that would bring together all three circles. Tell them each to put those choices in the space where the circles overlap.
- Provide a stack of used magazines, blank paper, and glue. Tell the girls each to tear out words and images that reflect their life's dreams and to create a collage. Suggest that they give their collage a place of honor, to remind themselves of the life they are called to live.
- Suggest that the girls interview older women about what their dreams were when they were teenagers. Encourage them to ask questions like these: "Did those dreams come true? If yes, how? If no, why not? Has your life been the one that wanted to live in you?"

Reflection and Discussion

Journal Questions

- ◎ Write down five dreams that you would accomplish if there were no obstacles—such as age, money, education, and time—in the way.
- ◎ Complete this sentence: "I think God is (or was) trying to tell me something about me when . . ."
- ◎ Find a large space where you can be alone. Put on your favorite piece of music and dance with your eyes closed. When you are done, write what you experienced, felt, and thought during your dance.
- ◎ Keep an ongoing dialogue between yourself and your life. To make the dialogue more real, you could even give your life a name. Start with the question posed at the beginning of this theme: "Is the life you are living the life that wants to live inside you?"

Scriptural Connections

- Wis. 6:12–25 (a description of wisdom)
- Wis. 7:23–30 (the nature of wisdom)
- Matt. 5:13–16 (being salt and light)
- John 4:7–15 (drinking deeply of the well of life)
- Phil. 3:12–16 (pressing on toward a goal)
- Col. 2:6–10 (living life to the fullest)

WomanWisdom Quotes

Often people attempt to live their lives backwards: they try to have more things, or more money, in order to do more of what they want so that they will be happier. The way it actually works is the reverse. You must first *be* who you really are, then, *do* what you need to do, in order to *have* what you want. (Margaret Young)

Nobody objects to a woman being a good writer or sculptor or geneticist if at the same time she manages to be a good wife, good mother, good-looking, good-tempered, well-groomed and unaggressive. (Leslie M. McIntyre)

To accept the responsibility of being a child of God is to accept the best that life has to offer you. (Stella Terrill Mann)

Not everyone's life is what they make it. Some people's life is what other people make it. (Alice Walker)

Your vocation? To complete the universe. (Pierre Teilhard de Chardin)

Prayers

Your time to be a little girl
won't come again.
That thought may be sad
for someone who doesn't know
how beautiful your youth
has been.
The memories of loving
and living will last forever
but now . . .
Your future as a woman
is even more exciting,
you are a masterpiece.
You go now, to bring beauty

to the world,
to be a strong woman
of great compassion.
As you step away, rejoice!
For whatever distance
comes between us,
I will share your days of sunshine
and help whisk away the clouds;
our hearts bound together
in a special love.
     (Hallie Wallen, "As You Grow")

When I am old and gray
with wrinkles spreading
from the corners of my
faded blue eyes,
I will think about
how I came to be
myself.
I will remember
all the struggles I faced.
I will think
about things I accomplished,
the people I met,
the lives I changed.
And then . . .
I will smile.
     (Anna M. Bruty, "Remembrance")

Resource Materials

Print

Kielbasa, Marilyn. *Stewardship: Creating the Future*. Horizons Program. Winona, MN: Saint Mary's Press, 1998. This is a three-session, 6-hour minicourse for older teens on stewardship, that is, the responsible management and application of the gifts of time, talent, and treasure.

Palmer, Parker J. *Let Your Life Speak: Listening for the Voice of Vocation*. San Francisco: Jossey-Bass Publishers, 2000. This is an unpretentious and well-written book about tuning out noisy preconceptions of what a vocation should and should not be, and creating the kind of quiet, trusting conditions that allow a soul to speak its truth.

Whitehead, Evelyn Eaton, and James D. Whitehead. *Seasons of Strength: New Visions of Adult Christian Maturing*. Winona, MN: Saint Mary's Press, 1995. This is a wonderful book for older teens, young adults, and adults, about discerning one's life path, achieving true maturity, and becoming the person God intended by living life to its fullest.

Notes

Use this space to jot ideas, reminders, and additional resources.

Circles of Friends

Promoting a Culture of Friendship

Springboard Activity

Ins and Outs in the World of Cliques

Girls often find themselves in confusing, hurtful, and painful relationships with their peers. This theme helps them to process their experiences with friends and cliques, name what is going on, and explore new and healthier ways of being in relationships with other girls.

Preparation
○ Bring in the Warner Studios movie *A Little Princess* (1995, 97 minutes, rated G).

1. Divide the girls into two groups. Give each girl a sheet of white construction paper, and crayons, markers, or colored pencils. Tell the girls in one group to write at the top of their paper the word, "Friendship," and the girls in the other group to write the word, "Cliques." Instruct the girls to spend 10 minutes drawing symbols or pictures that best illustrate their word.

2. When time is up, invite the girls to hang up their work around the room, leaving space around each paper. Then give each girl a pad of self-stick notes. Instruct everyone to view each paper without talking; to jot on a self-stick note their impressions, their thoughts, and any connections they make with the paper; and to post the note near the paper. (If your group is large, you may want to limit the number of papers the girls view, in the interest of time.)

3. After the girls have left their notes, go to all the papers that are about friendship and read aloud the comments on the corresponding notes. Then ask questions such as these:

◎ What images express your idea of friendship?

◎ Is friendship important to you? If so, why?

◎ What themes seem to connect all these papers? Why?

4. Go to all the papers about cliques and read aloud the comments on the notes for them. Then ask questions such as these:

◎ What images and themes appear in more than one paper? Why?

◎ How do cliques form? When do they start forming? Why?

5. Introduce the movie *A Little Princess* with comments like these:

◎ This movie, based on Frances Hodgson Burnett's novel by the same name, addresses the themes of friendship and cliques. When World War I breaks out and her father must serve as an officer in the British army, Sara Crewe leaves India to attend a boarding school. There, she encounters a stern and severe headmistress named Miss Minchin, who stifles her creativity and individuality. Sara learns much about herself, and the importance of friendships, as heartache, tragedy, and joy fill her life.

6. After the movie, use questions like these to help the girls discuss and process the story:

◎ How does Sara make friends?

◎ What kind of relationship does Sara form with the slave Becky? the snob Lavinia? the heavyset Ermengarde? little Lottie?

◎ How is Sara able to break through the cliques and show the girls what friendship is all about?

◎ How do storytelling, humor, and support bring the girls together?

Additional Activities

Femi-Jungle

1. Ask the group if they believe that girls and boys experience friendship and cliques differently. Challenge them to name all the differences they can think of, and write their responses on newsprint or the board.

2. Share the following information in your own words:

◎ I am now going to read several quotes from Jean Shepherd's book *In God We Trust, All Others Pay Cash*. The main character is Ralphie, a ten-year-old boy living in a small town. Shepherd describes the "jungle of kidhood" from his perspective. As I read the following passages, listen carefully and think about whether Ralphie's experiences as a boy match yours as a girl.

Then read the following excerpts:

- ◎ "The male human animal, skulking through the impenetrable fetid jungle of Kidhood, learns early in the game just what sort of animal he is. The jungle he stalks is a howling tangled wilderness, infested with crawling, flying, leaping, nameless dangers. There are occasional brilliant patches of rare, passionate orchids and other sweet flowers and succulent fruits, but they are rare. He daily does battle with horrors and emotions that he will spend the rest of his life trying to forget or suppress. Or recapture" (p. 112).

- ◎ "His jungle is a wilderness he will never fully escape. . . .
  "I am not at all sure that girls have even the slightest hint that there *is* such a jungle" (p. 112).

- ◎ "Every male child sweats inside at a word that is rarely heard today: the Bully. . . . Every school had at least five, and they usually gathered followers and toadies like barnacles on the bottom of a garbage scow. The lines were clearly drawn. You were either a Bully, a Toady, or one of the nameless rabble of Victims who hid behind hedges, continually ran up alleys, ducked under porches, and tried to get a connection with City Hall, City Hall being the Bully himself" (pp. 113–114).

When you are done, encourage the girls to share their impressions of the male jungle of kidhood and to discuss whether the author's descriptions of the jungle ring true just for boys.

3. Distribute handout 12, "The Queen Bee," and give the girls time to read the story on it individually. Then discuss how that story compares with the quotes from *In God We Trust*. Ask the girls to reflect on the power of individuals to affect the ecology of relationships in the jungle. Use questions like these to engage them in a discussion of that issue:

- ◎ How does the "femi-jungle" described in this story compare with the "kidhood jungle" of *In God We Trust?*
- ◎ Can you relate to any of the characters in this story? If so, which ones?
- ◎ How can one or two people in the subculture of peers have so much power over others?
- ◎ How does it feel to be inside a clique? outside a clique?
- ◎ What are the names and rules of some girl peer groups you know about? [It may be helpful to give examples from your own experience, such as the popular girls, the Barbie girls, and the tomboys.]

Surviving the Femi-Jungle and the Queen Bees

1. Offer the following comments in your own words:

- ◎ It can be a jungle out there! A jungle is dark and scary and full of threats. It is also full of life and beauty. Knowing the dangers and preparing to deal with them can make our experiences in the jungle of female relationships rewarding and memorable. What do you need in order to survive and thrive in the femi-jungle?

2. Divide the girls into three groups, give each group one of the following sets of items, and allow the groups time to complete the task outlined in their instructions:

- *Group 1.* a backpack, a collection of travel items, and these instructions:

   Directions. What do you need to survive the femi-jungle? Fill a backpack with what a girl needs in order to be a friend and make good friends and avoid destructive cliques. Use objects as symbols. For example, every girl needs a mirror to remind herself of who she is.

- *Group 2.* maps, blank paper, colored pencils or colored thin-line markers, and these instructions:

   Directions. How do you make your way through the femi-jungle? Draw a map that younger girls can use to navigate the jungle.

- *Group 3.* a travel guide; a blank booklet, blank paper, or newsprint; colored pencils or colored markers; and these instructions:

   Directions. Make a small booklet [or chart] of do's and don'ts for survival in the femi-jungle, addressing these questions: What must you do to be safe? What kind of risks should you take or avoid?

3. When the groups have completed their assigned tasks, invite them to share the results with everyone. Then ask the girls, "How could Sara and the other girls in the movie *The Little Princess* have used your travel advice?"

4. In conclusion, remind the girls of these things:
- ◉ Friendships can be life-giving, positive relationships that bring out the best in us.
- ◉ Cliques can be destructive and negative when exclusivity is their purpose.
- ◉ Boys and girls approach friendships differently.
- ◉ The femi-jungle can be threatening, but knowing how to navigate it can help us deal with the dangers.

Options and Actions

- For the springboard activity, if you do not have time to view the entire movie as a group, ask the girls to view it at home beforehand. When you meet, replay the scenes that are most relevant to the discussion of friendships and cliques.
- Encourage the girls to interview women of different ages and hear their stories of the femi-jungle. Ask the girls how those stories are similar to and different from their own and their peers'.
- Invite the girls to bring in music that speaks to them of healthy same-sex friendships. Discuss the lyrics, and share stories of friendship that are positive.

- Challenge the girls to draw a diagram of the social structure they live in, using stick figures to represent people and geometric shapes to symbolize groups. Divide the girls into small groups and ask everyone to explain their diagram to their group.
- Encourage your group to write their own prayers about friendship, including friendship with God. Or invite them to share music about friendship as a way to describe our relationship with Jesus. A good example is the classic James Taylor version of "You've Got a Friend."

Reflection and Discussion

Journal Questions

- How do you see yourself in relation to the femi-jungle of friendships and cliques? Describe or draw yourself in the jungle.
- Reflect on how you contribute positively or negatively to the ecological balance of your femi-jungle. In what ways are you life-giving? In what ways might you sometimes come across as a toxic hazard?

Scriptural Connections

- Ruth 1:16–18 (Ruth and Naomi)
- 1 Sam. 18:1–4 (Jonathan and David)
- Prov. 13:20 (walking with the wise)
- Prov. 22:24–25 (avoiding the angry and the hotheads)
- Sir. 6:5–17 (friendship, false and true)
- Sir. 9:10 (old friends)
- Phil. 1:3–11 (thanks for friends)

WomanWisdom Quotes

A friend can tell you things you don't want to tell yourself. (Frances Ward Weller)

Oh, the comfort—the inexpressible comfort of feeling *safe* with a person—having neither to weigh thoughts nor measure words, but pouring them all right out, just as they are, chaff and grain together; certain that a faithful hand will take and sift them, keep what is worth keeping, and then with the breath of kindness blow the rest away. (Dinah Maria Mulock Craik)

She is a friend of my mind. She gather me, man. The pieces I am, she gather them and give them back to me in all the right order. (Toni Morrison)

Friendship is a difficult, dangerous job. It is also (though we rarely admit it) extremely exhausting. (Elizabeth Bibesco)

Female friendships that work are relationships in which women help each other belong to themselves. (Louise Bernikow)

Prayer

You turned my darkness into light,
You made everything all right.
You picked me up when I was down,
You turned my life around.
If I didn't have you, what would I be?
A blessing is what you are to me.

When I needed you the most, you were there,
Even if it seemed like you didn't care.
When I didn't think I could make it another day,
You chased all my doubts away.
If I didn't have you, what would I be?
A treasure is what you are to me.

The world is full of many people, it's true,
But there is only one of you.
You fill my heart with love,
You're a God-sent gift from above.
If I didn't have you, what would I be?
An angel is what you are to me.

Lost and alone, I will no longer be,
Because you are here with me.
There is no reason to be sad,
You've taken away all the bad.
If I didn't have you, what would I be?
A best friend is what you are to me!
    (Katrina L. Troyer, "What You Mean to Me")

Resource Materials

Print

Saint Mary's Press. *The Catholic Youth Bible*. Winona, MN: Saint Mary's Press, 2000.
This Bible contains various articles on friendship that the girls might read and use
for reflection. See the *friendship* entry in the article subject index at the back of the
book.

Notes

Use the space below to jot ideas, reminders, and additional resources.

The Queen Bee

by Laurel Zimmerman

I know as soon as I leave first hour that Betta is up to her usual bull. I have to pass her and her pack in the hall by the math rooms, and for whatever reason, I get the snub. The snub is really subtle, very well done and finely honed. Not crude, like back in sixth grade, when Betta would call her two minions and tell them to call everyone and pass the word that tomorrow was Wear Red Day. Or Hat Day. Or Backwards Day. Except somebody just never got called. Sometimes it was me, sometimes it was someone else, sometimes two or three of us. Then, when we arrived at school, we were out of it. Occasionally, they made fun of us, but usually, they pretended that they had just screwed up and somebody forgot to call us. But of course, there we were, looking out of it. I have to admit it, and I feel guilty to say this, but when I *was* called, I felt relieved and almost, well, *grateful* to Betta in a weird way. Like, maybe she liked me! And sometimes she did, or acted as if she did. She had that thing about her, that she would be really mean, but then turn on the dazzle and be so nice to you that you just felt wonderful.

Anyway, that stuff shouldn't be bothering me now—not in high school. Wouldn't you think that we would be beyond it? But somehow, Betta's glitz and power followed her right into high school. I always had this image of her with those sprinkles all around her—just like in the Disney movie *Cinderella,* when the fairy godmothers keep changing the colors of Cinderella's dress. I can just see Betta swooping through the front door of school, with her handmaidens holding up her invisible, but very real, train of glamour.

Betta is the queen bee, and Brianne and Ali are her princesses. They fake it like they think they are her equals, but I can read the little tremors of nervousness just under the surface. She never really dumps on *them*—not exactly. She has to have *someone* to do the dirty work of propping up her regime. But sometimes she will just do little things. Like one time she confided in Ali about a fight with her current boyfriend, and didn't tell Brianne; she made sure that Brianne heard it thirdhand. Now, if you did that to a guy, he wouldn't think twice—what's the big deal? But Brianne was hurt, and more than that, scared. Brianne knew that without Betta, she was nada, zip, and that was truly scary. But she would never have confronted Betta. Way too risky. Better just hope she hadn't done anything to offend the queen bee. Lay low, be cool, be friendly, nothing has changed. Of course, the next time Betta needed to exert her power, she enveloped Brianne in her intimate exchanges of confidence, and Brianne could be relieved and, oh, yes, I'm certain, *grateful*. Let's face it—I can hack the baloney because I have other friends, and some really close ones. But Brianne has spent too much time working for Betta, and people are afraid of Betta and, by extension, Brianne and Ali. Those three really only have one another.

I get the lay of the land in the math hallway, and I watch them—Brianne, Ali, and Betta, and another couple of girls—and as I pass, I wonder, "Which technique will they use on me today?" They use silence. As I approach their territory, they are laughing and chatting merrily, but as I pass, they simply fall silent. They smile at me; some-one says, "Hello," in a friendly way. If you didn't get what was going on, like if you were a teacher, you would probably think it *is* friendly. But as I move away down the hall to second hour, they remain silent for just a beat, until I am far enough away, and then the peals of laughter resume, and the royalty continue their chatting.

Now, if you were real insecure, you might be forgiven if you worried about whether they are talking about you. But, of course, they are not. The whole thing is just part of one giant theatrical ploy to intimidate other girls, and so far in this life, it has worked.

Transforming Women
Promoting a Culture of Conversion

Springboard Activity

Changing the World, One Girl at a Time

This activity is recommended as a conclusion to the *Awakening* themes. It uses the movie *The Spitfire Grill* or *Beauty and the Beast* to encourage the girls to realize the power of women to transform the world. *The Spitfire Grill* is appropriate for those in their midteens and older; *Beauty and the Beast* is an alternative for younger girls. Both movies portray the main characters as intelligent, authentic heroines who bring healing and conversion to others, transforming their world.

Preparation

○ Bring in an assortment of items associated with change, such as a tire, a diaper, a bedsheet or pillowcase, underwear or other clothes, paint chips, coins, a lightbulb, nail polish, an oil filter, a package of yeast or gelatin, food coloring, a leaf, a "transformer toy," and a caterpillar. Arrange these on a table.

○ Bring in a heart of some kind (to symbolize a change of heart), a picture or sculpture of a head (to symbolize a change of mind), and a small globe (to symbolize a change of the world).

○ Review and bring in the movie *The Spitfire Grill* (Castle Rock, 1996, 116 minutes, rated PG-13) or *Beauty and the Beast* (Walt Disney, 1991, 84 minutes, rated G), depending on the age of the girls in your group. As you watch the movie, keep in mind the questions in step 5 of this activity plan.

○ Consider bringing in stuffed monkeys as visual aids for the story in step 7.

1. Gather the girls around the table with the assortment of items and ask them what those items have in common. You might award one or more of the objects to the girl or girls who correctly name the common characteristic as change.

2. Engage the group in a short discussion about change, using questions like the ones that follow:

- ◉ When is change good? bad?
- ◉ What kinds of changes are easy to achieve?
- ◉ What makes change difficult to achieve sometimes?
- ◉ What change have you made that was hard but worth it?

3. Add the symbols for change of heart and change of mind to the table. Note that conversion involves both the head and the heart. Explain that it is a process of turning toward God with "the desire and resolution to change one's life, with hope in God's mercy and trust in the help of [God's] grace" (*Catechism,* no. 1431).

4. Introduce *The Spitfire Grill* or *Beauty and the Beast,* and its theme of change and conversion. Encourage the girls to watch for examples of how the characters change or experience conversion. Show the movie.

5. Using the appropriate set of questions and comments below, lead a discussion about the development of the main characters from the movie and how they each experience change.

The Spitfire Grill

- ◉ How do Percy, Hannah, and Shelby help and empower one another to change? How does the way that they use their voices change?
- ◉ How do these women help or empower the other characters in the film? As these women change, how do others around them change?
- ◉ Shelby sings the following verse of a traditional religious song:

> There is a balm in Gilead
> to make the wounded whole,
> there is a balm in Gilead
> to heal the sin-sick soul
> ("There Is a Balm in Gilead")

  Balm is an ointment that heals or soothes, and Gilead is a place mentioned in the Bible (Jer. 8:22) where conflicts often happen. Why is the song significant to the message of the movie?

- ◉ How did you feel when Percy told her story of incest, violence, and manslaughter? How did Percy feel about her unborn child? her crime? Why is it significant that she tells this story in church?
- ◉ In the Bible, Jesus says, "No one has greater love than this, to lay down one's life for one's friends" (John 15:13). How does Percy become a Christ figure in the movie?
- ◉ How do Shelby's life and death bring change and healing to the wounded souls in Gilead?
- ◉ Why, do you think, does Hannah choose Claire to buy the Spitfire Grill?

Beauty and the Beast

- Describe Belle's personality. What makes her special?
- Compare Belle with Ariel in the movie *The Little Mermaid.*
- Do people like or dislike Belle because of her beauty? How important are looks to a person's popularity? Are looks more important for girls than for boys? Can beauty or good looks ever be a disadvantage?
- What qualities of Belle's help her to see beyond the ugliness of the Beast?
- Jesus says, "No one has greater love than this, to lay down one's life for one's friends" (John 15:13). How is Belle willing to do that?

6. Put the term, "Transformation," on newsprint or the board and ask its meaning. Define the word as "a thorough and fundamental change in the appearance or nature of a thing or person." Then present questions like these for discussion:

- How does this term relate to change or conversion?
- How does it apply to the film?
- How is forgiveness an essential part of change, conversion, or transformation? Use examples from the movie to explain your answer.

Add the globe to the table of change items, and continue the discussion with questions like these:

- How do the women in the movie transform the world around them?
- Can you think of other women who make or have made change happen? Consider the women in your family, parish, school, or community, in the nation, and in the world.

7. Tell the following story, using stuffed monkeys as visual aids if you so desire:

The Hundredth Monkey

Off the shore of Japan, scientists had been studying monkey colonies on many separate islands for over thirty years. In order to keep track of the monkeys, they would lure them out of the trees by dropping sweet potatoes on the beach. The monkeys came to enjoy this free lunch, and were in plain sight where they could be observed. One day, an eighteen-month-old female monkey named Imo started to wash her sweet potato in the sea before eating it. I imagine that it tasted better without the grit and sand or pesticides, or maybe it even was slightly salty and that was good. Imo showed her playmates and her mother how to do this, her friends showed their mothers, and gradually more and more monkeys began to wash their sweet potatoes instead of eating them grit and all. At first, only the female adults who imitated their children learned, but gradually others did also.

One day, the scientists observed that all the monkeys on that particular island washed their sweet potatoes before eating them. Although this was significant, what was even more fascinating was that this change in monkey behavior did not take place only on this one island. Suddenly, the monkeys on all the other islands were now washing their sweet potatoes as well—despite the fact that monkey colonies on the different islands had no direct contact with each other. (Ken Keyes Jr., as retold in Jean Shinoda Bolen, *The Millionth Circle,* pp. 11–12)

Ask the girls how the story and the movie relate. Then present the following ideas in your own words:

- ◎ "The Hundredth Monkey" shows how change occurs in a group. When a critical number of people change their attitude or behavior, culture at large will change.
- ◎ Each of us can choose to change our culture in positive ways. We may be the first monkey, or more likely the fiftieth. For human culture to change, there has to be a human equivalent of Imo and her friends.
- ◎ The world desperately needs the wisdom and compassion that are associated with the feminine aspects of humanity. The world will change through women who together speak, listen, laugh, cry, and share their knowledge, insight, and judgment.

8. Consider ending with a prayer service incorporating elements from the film. For *The Spitfire Grill,* use scented water (to symbolize balm), and have the girls write letters about why they might or might not want to own a place like the Spitfire Grill. Also play or sing the hymn "There Is a Balm in Gilead," which is available in many hymnals.

If the group viewed *Beauty and the Beast,* give each girl a rose, to celebrate God's grace within her, and a book or a journal, to celebrate her intelligence. Use the movie's title song, "Beauty and the Beast," and lead a reflection about the spiritual message of the movie—the triumph of grace and goodness over sin.

Options and Actions

- Celebrate local women who have worked for change, by inviting them to a special meal. At the gathering, tell the story "The Hundredth Monkey" and give each honoree her own stuffed monkey as a memento.
- Give each girl a pebble. Arrange the group in a circle and place a large shallow bowl or tub of water in the center of the circle, or gather outside near a pond or other body of water. Invite each girl to toss her pebble into the water, watch the concentric circles that flow out from the place where it hits the water, and share something she has done that may have had a positive effect on the world around her or something she would like to do to change the world.
- On separate slips of paper, write the names of women in history or the Bible who have been change agents, and place the slips in a container. Have each girl draw one slip, research the person named on it, and prepare a short presentation for the group. The girls might dress like their subject and tell her story in the first person.
- Discuss ways that circles of girls or women have the power to change the world. Name some circles that the girls belong to, such as Girl Scouts and service groups. Brainstorm ways that girls and women can form circles that bring about positive transformations in the world. Also discuss situations in which circles of girls and women can have a negative influence in the world, such as cliques or gangs.

- There are many biblical references in *The Spitfire Grill:* the name of the town (Gilead), the names of characters (Hannah and Eli), and so forth. Use a concordance or Bible encyclopedia to find the significance of those names, or ask the girls to do so.
- In the scriptural connections for this theme, Jesus engages women in the message of God's Reign, the transformation of the world. Each of those women is marginalized by her gender in a patriarchal world, and is suspect for other reasons as well. Read the biblical stories with the girls, and help them to draw comparisons between the biblical figures and the movie characters.
- Organize a club to watch movies about strong women who use their gifts of wisdom, compassion, and creativity to bring about transformation. Or lead the girls in writing reviews of movies with transforming women, for a local or school paper.
- If your group watched *The Spitfire Grill,* also show *Beauty and the Beast,* and then ask the girls to compare Percy with Belle, posing questions like these:
  - What do they have in common?
  - How do they both befriend "beasts" and choose goodness in the face of violence?
- Have older teens lead younger girls in a viewing and discussion of *Beauty and the Beast,* using the process described in the springboard activity.

Reflection and Discussion

Journal Questions

- Think about ways that you might challenge the culture and promote transformation in the world. Reflect on and write about the gifts you have that you might use to change the world—perhaps as a writer, artist, speaker, actress, athlete, adventurer, engineer, mechanic, mother, sister, or friend.
- If you had the power to change any aspect of your world, what would it be?
- In what ways could you be a balm in your parish, school, family, or community?
- What transformations need to take place in your own mind and heart for you to live more fully?

Scriptural Connections

- Matt. 15:21–28 or Mark 7:25 (Canaanite or Syrophoenician woman)
- Mark 5:25–34 (woman with hemorrhages)
- Luke 7:36–50 (sinful woman who anoints Jesus)
- John 4:1–42 (Samaritan woman at the well)
- John 7:53—8:11 (adulterous woman)

WomanWisdom Quotes

Never doubt that a small group of thoughtful, committed citizens can change the world; indeed, it is the only thing that ever has. (Margaret Mead)

What will not change is the presence of God, who leads us always to more and more awareness, more and more life. (Joan D. Chittister)

It is your business and others' to go forth, confronting them face to face, for that is the only way of bringing them to Me. For when you are face to face with them, you love them, and once you love them, then I can speak through you. (Catherine de Hueck Doherty)

Start with women's circles,
each one is like a pebble thrown in a pond.
· · · · · · · · · · · · ·
If enough women learn from each other,
and change their behavior,
like Imo and her friends,
in the story of The Hundredth Monkey,
the way things are done and what is believed
can change.
                    (Jean Shinoda Bolen)

To the young women of the church we say: Carry forward the cause of gospel feminism. We will be with you along the way, sharing what we have learned about the freedom, joy and power of contemplative intimacy with God. We ask you to join us in a commitment to far-reaching transformation of church and society in non-violent ways. (Madeleva Manifesto)

Prayer

I yearned to see heaven,
And God showed it to me.
I yearned to feel love,
And God gave it to me,
I yearned to be cared for,
And God cared for me.
I yearned for compassion,
And God gave it to me.
I yearned for forgiveness,
And God forgave me.
I yearned to know what God wanted of me,

And God said,
> Go likewise and do for others
> What I have done for you.
> (Amanda Maisonneuve, "My Calling")

Resource Materials

Print

Bolen, Jean Shinoda. *The Millionth Circle: How to Change Ourselves and the World.* Berkeley, CA: Conari Press, 1999. This book is based on the theory of the hundredth monkey: that a behavioral change in a growing number of individuals will reach critical mass and impact the consciousness of the entire population. The author's theory is that the millionth women's circle will alter the patriarchal psyche of the human race.

Covey, Sean. *The Seven Habits of Highly Effective Teens: The Ultimate Teenage Success Guide.* New York: Simon and Schuster, 1998. In this book, the author applies the timeless principles captured in his father's book, *The Seven Habits of Highly Effective People,* to teenagers and the tough issues and life-changing decisions they face.

Covey, Stephen R. *The Seven Habits of Highly Effective People: Restoring the Character Ethic.* New York: Simon and Schuster, 1989. The author in this book presents a holistic, integrated, principle-centered approach for solving personal and professional problems, adapting to change, and taking advantage of the opportunities that change creates.

Notes

Use this space to jot ideas, reminders, and additional resources.

Acknowledgments *(continued from page 4)*

The scriptural quotations contained herein are from the New Revised Standard Version of the Bible. Copyright © 1989 by the Division of Christian Education of the National Council of the Churches of Christ in the United States of America. All rights reserved.

The first, second, fourth, and fifth guidelines listed on page 14 are paraphrased from *Beyond Nice: The Spiritual Wisdom of Adolescent Girls,* by Patricia H. Davis (Minneapolis: Fortress Press, 2001), pages 119, 120, 121, and 121, respectively. Copyright © 2001 by Augsburg Fortress.

The statistics on page 24 are from Education Now, Oxfam America, as given at *www.oxfamamerica.org.*

The words of Anna Julia Cooper and Eleanor Roosevelt on page 25 and of Simone de Beauvoir on page 83 are quoted from *In Celebration of Women: A Selection of Words and Paintings,* by Helen Exley (New York: Exley Publications LLC, 1996). Copyright © 1996 by Helen Exley. All rights reserved.

The words of Boutros Boutros-Ghali on page 25 are quoted from *www.un.org/ Conferences/Women/PubInfo/Status/Home.htm,* 13 November 2000.

The words of Arthur John Gossip on page 25 are quoted from *Topical Encyclopedia of Living Quotations,* edited by Sherwood Eliot Wirt and Kersten Beckstrom (Minneapolis: Bethany House Publishers, 1982), page 258. Copyright © 1982 by Sherwood Wirt and Kersten Beckstrom.

The words of Anasuya Sengupta on page 25; Antoinette Brown Blackwell on page 37; Carmen Martínez Ten, Sheila Rowbotham, Alix Kates Shulman, and Kate Millett on page 51; Pauline Kael and Jessamyn West on page 69; Pearl Cleage and Anita Hill on page 84; Etty Hillesum on page 98; Audre Lorde, Madeleine Kunin, and Maude Royden on page 108; Alice Walker on page 116; and Frances Ward Weller, Dinah Maria Mulock Craik, Toni Morrison, Elizabeth Bibesco, and Louise Bernikow on page 122 are quoted from *The New Beacon Book of Quotations by Women,* compiled by Rosalie Maggio (Boston: Beacon Press, 1996), pages 750; 753; 381, 382, 624, and 625; 10 and 38; 566 and 625–626; 352; 542, 513, and 114; 402; and 271, 270, 270, 272, and 272; respectively. Copyright © 1996 by Rosalie Maggio. All rights reserved.

The words of Tim Hinds Flinders and Carol Lee Flinders on page 26 are quoted from, the fourth option on page 35 is adapted from, and the findings of Susan Harter on pages 39–40 are reported from *Power and Promise: Helping Schoolgirls Hold onto Their Dreams,* by Tim Hinds Flinders with Carol Lee Flinders, PhD (Petaluma, CA: Two Rock Publications, 1999), pages 49, 206 (activity 3), and 36. Copyright © 1999 by Timothy Hinds Flinders and Carol Lee Flinders, PhD. Used with permission by the author. All rights reserved.

The words of Carol Lee Flinders on page 37 are quoted from her *At the Root of This Longing: Reconciling a Spiritual Hunger and a Feminist Thirst* ([San Francisco]: HarperSanFrancisco, 1998), page 313. Copyright © 1998 by Carol Lee Flinders.

The prayers on pages 37, 38, 69–70, 84, 116–117, 124, and 133–134 are from *Listen for a Whisper: Prayers, Poems, and Reflections by Girls,* edited by Janet Claussen and Marilyn Kielbasa (Winona, MN: Saint Mary's Press, 2001), pages 69, 161, 88, 149, 166, 66, and 29, respectively. Copyright © 2001 by Saint Mary's Press. All rights reserved.

Nancy R. Smith's poem "For Every Woman," on handout 2, is excerpted from *Images of Women in Transition,* compiled by Janice Grana (Winona, MN: Saint Mary's Press, 1991), page 49. Copyright © 1976 by The Upper Room, Nashville, Tennessee. All rights reserved. Used with permission of Upper Room Books.

The definition of *feminism* on page 44 is quoted from *The Random House Dictionary of the English Language,* college edition, 1968.

The definition of *Gospel feminism* on pages 44–45 is quoted from *With Oil in Their Lamps: Faith, Feminism, and the Future,* 2000 Madeleva lecture in spirituality, by Sandra M. Schneiders (New York: Paulist Press, 2000), page 116. Copyright © 2000 by Saint Mary's College, Notre Dame, Indiana.

The leader comments in step 3 on pages 49–50 are adapted from *The Catholic Youth Bible,* by Saint Mary's Press (Winona, MN: Saint Mary's Press, 2000), page 810. Copyright © 2000 by Saint Mary's Press. All rights reserved.

The activity "Sexism in the Scriptures," on pages 49–50 is adapted from "Sexism Reversal," in *Teaching Activities Manual for* The Catholic Youth Bible, by Christine Schmertz Navarro et al. (Winona, MN: Saint Mary's Press, 2000), pages 139–140. Copyright © 2000 by Saint Mary's Press. All rights reserved.

The words of Cecilia Mitchell on pages 51 and 108 are from *Wisdom's Daughters: Conversations with Women Elders of Native America,* by Steve Wall, as reprinted in *In Celebration of Women,* by Helen Exley. Copyright © 1993 by Steve Wall. Used with permission of HarperCollins Publishers, Inc.

The words of Pope John Paul II on page 52 are from his encyclical *The Gospel of Life* (*Evangelium Vitae,* 1995), number 99, as quoted in *Origins,* 6 April 1995, volume 24, number 42, page 723. Copyright © 1995 by Catholic News Service.

The words of the Madeleva Manifesto on page 53, on resource 5, and on page 133 are quoted from a sidebar to "'Coloring Outside the Patriarchal Lines,'" by Patrick Marrin, *National Catholic Reporter,* 12 May 2000.

The words of Patricia McGuire on page 53 are paraphrased from, and on resource 5 are quoted from her 2000 speech "Transforming the Political and Social Discourse of Our Times," as quoted in *Origins,* 13 April 2000, volume 29, number 43, pages 705 and 704. Copyright © 2000 by Catholic News Service.

The extract on handout 3 is adapted from "The Good Wife's Guide," *Housekeeping Monthly,* 13 May 1955.

The words of Pope Pius XII on resource 4 are from his 1941 "Allocution to Newly-Weds," paragraph 82, as quoted in *Women Christian: New Vision,* by Mary T. Malone (Dubuque, IA: Brown ROA Publishing Media, 1985), page 1. Copyright © 1985 by Wm. C. Brown Co. Publishers.

On resource 5, the words of the U.S. Bishops' Committee on Women in Society and in the Church, and of Diana Hayes are quoted from *The Wisdom of Women: Models for Faith and Action,* by the U.S. Bishops' Committee on Women in Society and in the Church, National Conference of Catholic Bishops (NCCB) (Washington, DC: United States Catholic Conference [USCC], 1991), pages 27 and 28. Copyright © 1991 by the USCC.

The statement of Pope John Paul II that begins "Women have a full right" on resource 5 is from his message "Women: Teachers of Peace," as quoted in *Origins,* 22 December 1994, volume 24, number 28, pages 468–469. Copyright © 1994 by Catholic News Service.

The statement of Pope John Paul II that begins "I make an appeal" on resource 5 is from his 1995 "Appeal to the Church on Women's Behalf," as quoted in *Origins,* 7 September 1995, volume 25, number 12, page 187. Copyright © 1995 by Catholic News Service.

The words of the U.S. Bishops on resource 5 are from their 1994 reflection "Strengthening the Bonds of Peace," as quoted in *Origins,* 1 December 1994, volume 24, number 25, pages 420–421. Copyright © 1994 by Catholic News Service.

On resource 5, Archbishop Alex Brunett's paraphrasing of the *Catechism,* Brunett's words of apology, and Aung San Suu Kyi's words are from Brunett's 2000 liturgy "The Ways Women Follow Christ," as quoted in *Origins,* 13 April 2000, volume 29, number 43, pages 706–707, 706, and 708, respectively. Copyright © 2000 by Catholic News Service.

All other quotes on resources 4 and 5 are from *Called into Her Presence: Praying with Feminine Images of God,* by Virginia Ann Froehle, RSM (Notre Dame, IN: Ave Maria Press, 1992), pages 127–130. Copyright © 1992 by Ave Maria Press, Notre Dame, IN 46556. Used with permission of author. All rights reserved.

Most of the facts on pages 63–64 are from; the quote in step 1 on page 67 is from; and some of the background information on page 71 is paraphrased and quoted from *Deadly Persuasion: Why Women and Girls Must Fight the Addictive Power of Advertising,* by Jean Kilbourne (New York: Free Press, 1999), pages 58, 133, and 133; 271; and 58, 129, and 130; respectively. Copyright © 1999 by Jean Kilbourne.

One of the facts on page 63, and the first, second, fourth, fifth, and sixth facts listed on page 99 are from a brochure published by the Atlanta Anti-Eating Disorders League, 1640 Powers Ferry Road, Building 7, Suite 300, Marietta, Georgia 30067, 770-953-4744 x-13 (phone), 770-953-4640 (fax), *psycinfo@mindspring.com, www.aaedl.com.*

The activity "Images of Media Women," on page 65, and the behavior lists on handout 6 are adapted from *Break the Lies that Bind: Sexism in the Media,* by the Center for Media Literacy (Los Angeles: Center for Media Literacy, 1994), page 28. Copyright © 1990 by the Center for Media Literacy. Used with permission. All rights reserved.

The activity "Monitoring the News," on pages 66–67, is adapted from "How to Conduct a Gender Study of Your Local Newspaper," by the Center for Media and Values, *Media and Values,* winter 1989, number 49, page 13. Copyright © 1989 by the Center for Media and Values. Used with permission.

The last option and action on page 68 is adapted from "Using Rock Videos to Analyze MTV," by Myra Junyk, *Media and Values*, winter 1989, number 49, page 19. Copyright © 1989 by the Center for Media and Values. Used with permission.

The words of Roseanne Arnold on page 69 are quoted from *A Century of Women*, edited by Alan Covey (Atlanta: TBS Books, 1994), page 178. Copyright © 1994 by Turner Publishing.

The words of Pierre Teilhard de Chardin on page 72 are quoted from his text *The Divine Milieu: An Essay on the Interior Life* (New York: Harper and Brothers, 1960), page 35. English translation copyright © 1960 by William Collins Sons, London, and Harper and Brothers, New York. All rights reserved.

The questions on handout 5 are adapted from, the first leader comment in step 3 on page 79 is paraphrased from, the last fact listed in step 2 on page 79 is from, and the facts listed on page 86 are from *Body Wars: Making Peace with Women's Bodies*, by Margo Maine, PhD (Carlsbad, CA: Gürze Books, 2000), pages 83, 152, 152, and 151–152, respectively. Copyright © 2000 by Margo Maine, PhD.

The activity "Recognizing and Naming Sexual Harassment," on pages 75–78 is adapted from; the activity "Sexual Harassment: Assumptions and Attitudes," on page 80 is adapted from; parts of the leader comments in step 2 on page 81 are adapted from; some of the background information on pages 85–87 is quoted and paraphrased from; the list on handout 9 is quoted from; and the process on handout 10 is adapted from *Sexual Harassment and Teens: A Program for Positive Change*, by Susan Strauss with Pamela Espeland (Minneapolis: Free Spirit Publishing, 1992), pages 44–47 and 107–108; 74 and 97; 98, 68, and 99–100; 19 and 3; 117; and 118; respectively. Copyright © 1992 by Susan Strauss. Used with permission from FreeSpirit Publishers Inc., Minneapolis, MN; 1-800-735-7323; www.freespirit.com. All rights reserved.

On page 78, the first definition of *violence* is quoted from and the definition of *domestic violence* is adapted from *Christian Justice: Sharing God's Goodness*, by Julia Ahlers and Michael Wilt (Winona, MN: Saint Mary's Press, 1995), pages 101 and 195. Copyright © 1995 by Saint Mary's Press. All rights reserved.

The first fact listed in step 2 on page 79 is quoted from and the second fact is adapted from "Rape Facts II," at *www.rape101.com/handouts/rape_facts_ii.htm*, 9 November 2000.

The third, fourth, and fifth facts listed in step 2 on page 79 are adapted from "Date Rape," at *www.rape101.com/handouts/date_rape.htm*, 8 November 2000.

The activity "Resisting Pressure," on page 82 is adapted from *The Underground Guide to Teenage Sexuality*, by Michael J. Basso, as excerpted at "Resisting Pressure to Have Sex," *www.rape101.com/resisting_pressure_to_have_sex.htm*, 8 November 2000. Copyright © 1997 Michael J. Basso. Used with permission of Fairview Press, www.fairviewpress.org

The words of the U.S. Bishops on page 87 are quoted from *When I Call for Help: A Pastoral Response to Domestic Violence Against Women*, by their Committees on Marriage and Family Life and on Women in Society and in the Church (Washington, DC: NCCB, USCC, Secretariat for Family, Laity, Women and Youth, 1992), as quoted at *www.nccbuscc.org/laity/help.htm*, 5 December 2000.

The words of Pope John Paul II on page 87 are from his apostolic letter *On the Dignity and Vocation of Women (Mulieris Dignitatem,* 1989), as quoted in *When I Call for Help,* by the U.S. Bishops' Committees on Marriage and Family Life and on Women in Society and in the Church.

The opening extract on handout 7 is adapted from *Growing in Christian Morality,* by Julia Ahlers, Barbara Allaire, and Carl Koch (Winona, MN: Saint Mary's Press, 1992), page 204. Copyright © 1992 by Saint Mary's Press. All rights reserved.

The building blocks on handout 7 are adapted from "Four Building Blocks in Understanding Teen Dating Violence," at *www.rape101.com/handouts/understanding_teen_dating_violence.htm,* 9 November 2000.

The table on handout 8 is adapted from *I Never Called It Rape: The Ms. Report on Recognizing, Fighting, and Surviving Date and Acquaintance Rape,* by Robin Warshaw, as excerpted at "Myths About Acquaintance Rape," *www.rape101.com/myths.htm,* 8 November 2000. Copyright © 1988 by the Ms. Foundation for Education and Communication, Inc., and Sarah Lazin Books. Reprinted with permission of Harper-Collins Publishers, Inc. All rights reserved.

The words of Billy Joel on page 98 are from his lyrics for "Just the Way You Are," copyright © 1977 by Impulsive Music, as quoted in *Chicken Soup for the Woman's Soul: 101 Stories to Open the Hearts and Rekindle the Spirits of Women,* by Jack Canfield et al. (Deerfield Beach, FL: Health Communications, 1996), page 75. Copyright © 1996 by Jack Canfield, Mark Victor Hansen, Jennifer Read Hawthorne, and Marci Shimoff.

The words of Mother Teresa on page 98 are quoted from *Chicken Soup for the Woman's Soul,* by Jack Canfield et al.

The seventh fact listed on page 100 is from "About-Face Facts on the Media," compiled by Liz Dittrich, PhD, at *www.about-face.org/resources/facts/media.html,* 3 November 2000. Copyright © 1998 by About-Face.

The eighth fact listed on page 100 is from "General Information on Eating Disorders," by the American Anorexia Bulimia Association, at *www.aabainc.org/general/index.html,* 3 November 2000.

The eleventh fact listed on page 100 is from the National Institute of Mental Health, as quoted at *www.aabainc.org,* 3 November 2000.

The twelfth fact listed on page 100 is from "About-Face Facts on SES, Ethnicity, and the Thin Ideal," compiled by Liz Dittrich, PhD, at *www.about-face.org/resources/facts/ses.html,* 3 November 2000.

The extracts on resource 6 are quoted from *Out of the Mouths of Babes: A Study of the Perceptions of Adolescent Girls,* by Laurel Zimmerman, EdD (doctoral dissertation, University of Saint Thomas, March 1994), pages 80, 48, 70, 77, 79, 29, 31, and 84, respectively. Used with permission of author.

Kathleen Fraser's "Poem in Which My Legs Are Accepted," on handout 11, is quoted from *Women in Literature: Life Stages Through Stories, Poems, and Plays,* by Sandra Eagleton, PhD (Englewood Cliffs, NJ: Prentice-Hall, 1988), pages 109–110. Copyright © 1988 by Prentice-Hall, Inc. All rights reserved.

The words of Parker J. Palmer on page 113 are quoted from his *Let Your Life Speak: Listening for the Voice of Vocation* (San Francisco: Jossey-Bass Publishers, 2000), front flap. Copyright © 2000 by Jossey-Bass Publishers.

The words of Margaret Young, Leslie M. McIntyre, and Stella Terrill Mann on page 116 are quoted from *The Artist's Way: A Spiritual Path to Higher Creativity,* by Julia Cameron (New York: Jeremy P. Tarcher/Putnam, 1992), pages 96, 99, and 104, respectively. Copyright © 1992 by Julia Cameron.

The three excerpts on page 121 are from *In God We Trust, All Others Pay Cash,* by Jean Shepherd (New York: Doubleday, 1966), pages 112, 112, and 113–114, respectively. Copyright © 1966 by Jean Shepherd.

The quote in step 3 on page 129 is from the *Catechism of the Catholic Church,* second edition, by the Libreria Editrice Vaticana, translated by the USCC (Washington, DC: USCC, 1997), number 1431. English translation of the Catechism of the Catholic Church for the United States of America copyright © 1994 by the USCC—Libreria Editrice Vaticana. English translation of the Catechism of the Catholic Church: Modifications from the Editio Typica copyright © 1997 by the USCC—Libreria Editrice Vaticana.

The lyrics from "There Is a Balm in Gilead" on page 129 are quoted from *Today's Missal: Breaking Bread Edition,* large print, by Oregon Catholic Press, 29 November 1998–25 November 1999, volume 66, number 2, hymn 548. Copyright © 1993 by Oregon Catholic Press.

The story on page 130, the words of Margaret Mead on page 133, and the words of Jean Shinoda Bolen on page 133 are quoted from *The Millionth Circle: How to Change Ourselves and the World,* by Jean Shinoda Bolen, MD (Berkeley, CA: Conari Press, 1999), pages 11–12, 80, and 84–85, respectively. Copyright © 1999 by Jean Shinoda Bolen, MD, by permission of Conari Press.

The words of Joan D. Chittister on page 133 are quoted from her *Heart of Flesh: A Feminist Spirituality for Women and Men* (Grand Rapids, MI: William B. Eerdmans Publishing; jointly with Ottawa: Novalis, Saint Paul University, 1998), page 11. Text copyright © 1998 by William B. Eerdmans Publishing Co.

The words of Catherine de Hueck Doherty on page 133 are quoted from *Soul Weavings: A Gathering of Women's Prayers,* edited by Lyn Klug (Minneapolis: Augsburg Fortress, 1996), page 99. Copyright © 1996 by Augsburg Fortress.